Juggling It All

The SHE guide to your work, your children
and your life

SARAH KILBY

EBURY PRESS
LONDON

To Anna-Louise

Published in 1992 by Vermilion
an imprint of Ebury Press
Random House
20 Vauxhall Bridge Road
London SW1V 2SA

A catalogue record for this book is
available from the British Library

ISBN 0 09 177341 5

Designed by Rowan Seymour
Typeset in Linotron Sabon by
Rowland Phototypesetting Ltd
Bury St Edmunds, Suffolk
Printed and bound in Great Britain by
Mackays of Chatham plc, Chatham, Kent

CONTENTS

Acknowledgements

Many thanks to all the working mothers and carers who gave so generously of their valuable time and experience to contribute to this book, especially those who welcomed me into their homes, opened bottles of wine and talked into the night. I am indebted also to those who contributed their expertise in other areas, in particular Chris Davies of the Return Consultancy, Georgina Corscadden, Lucy Daniels of the Working Mothers' Association, Jan Burnell and Kay Lyons of the National Childminding Association, Collette Kelleher of the Kids' Club Network, Susan Wasmuth of the Pre-Select Nanny Agency, and Jane Harris Matthews of the National Nursery Examination Board. No working mother should neglect her support network—my thanks go to Tina Hamshaw and her family, the staff of Toots Nursery, to Vicki Cohen for stepping into the breach, to Annie Shone for intrepid research and unflagging encouragement and to Alexander, without whom I could never have become a working mother in the first place!

Foreword

I returned to full-time work when my son was just three months old. By the time I became editor of SHE Magazine at the end of 1989, Thomas was one and a half, and the mayhem was beginning to subside. Nanny number four (boy, was I a bad judge of character in the early days) was a gem and Thomas was only waking up about twice a night (that might not sound good to you but it was a great improvement on his earlier record). And because Thomas waved me off happily each morning and greeted me with warm kisses each evening as I returned from work, I was feeling about as guilt-free as it's possible for any working mother to be . . .

I arrived at SHE with a mission – a mission to produce the first glossy magazine that celebrated motherhood and celebrated self under one umbrella. A magazine that would campaign vigorously on behalf of working mothers, by lobbying employers and government alike on subjects ranging from childcare to flexible working. A magazine that would support working mothers by guiding them through their rights and their options. A magazine that, through its pages, would enable working mothers to share their experiences – the good and the bad. A magazine that would focus on helping women to get the balance right in their busy, often frantic, lives. A magazine that would talk not about having it all (the superwoman myth), but about juggling it all – job, children, partner, home – as successfully as possible.

This book is the result of the kind of questions we at SHE are constantly asked by mothers wherever we go.

'How on earth do you manage?' 'What should I look out for when interviewing a childminder?' 'How do you think my boss will react if I bring up the question of job-sharing?' 'How long do you think I should take off?' 'Should I lie to my boss and call in sick when it's really my child who is unwell?' 'Do all mothers feel guilty, or is it only me?' 'Will I ever get a minute for myself?'

Sarah Kilby, herself a working mother and regular contributor to SHE, has answered all these questions and a myriad more in her exhaustive research for this book. She has interviewed literally hundreds of working mothers and passes on to you the wisdom of their experiences – and their mistakes.

A fact of life today is that the majority of mothers work. According to the General Household Survey 1989 (the latest statistics available) 63 per cent of women with dependent children are economically active. Whilst the majority of mothers still work part-time – especially those whose youngest child is still under four – more women are returning to full-time work, and doing it sooner, than ever before. Society, however, has not geared itself up to the dramatic changes that have taken place in women's lives and information is not easily to hand.

This book can't do the juggling for you, but it will certainly point you in the right direction. And if you're in need of a confidence boost, you need look no further than these pages.

I've learned to take pride in the fact that I juggle my life. I hope, with the help of this book, that you will, too.

Linda Kelsey
Editor
SHE

Preface

If you are contemplating the prospect of combining work and motherhood you will be hungry for information. Part One contains a wealth of practical and emotional advice to help you get through pregnancy, maternity leave and your return to work, and to help you decide what types of childcare are right for you and your child, from birth to teenage independence. Also, by probing the issues more deeply than has been done previously, it examines the delicate nature of the relationship between mother and carer. There are frank and sometimes shocking observations from both sides, which no working mother can afford to ignore.

In Part Two the focus is on you. Making life easier should be the motto of every working mother—here you will find the practical help to do so. There's a no-need-to-think cookery section, including a stress-free guide to entertaining, plus a too-tired-to-think party planner for birthday bashes. You'll feel better if you can squeeze in some time purely for yourself. There are plenty of ideas for recharging your batteries, with or without your partner, but definitely *sans* kids! Feeling and looking good will also help you cope; if you protest that there's no time in your schedule for exercise, try the amazing 12-minute tone-up on page 150.

Part Three looks to the future, examining new working patterns which could help working parents. If you are struggling with the nine-to-five hassle, sound out your boss on some of the alternatives. Take inspiration from the women who gritted their teeth and renegotiated their contracts to suit themselves and their families. Confidence is also a problem for women returning to work after a break. If you feel more trepidation than anticipation about *your* future then consult Chapter 12. You might want to approach some of the more go-ahead companies who are showing initiative, in the way of retraining schemes and helpful childcare arrangements. Chapter 13 looks at a few leading lights—could the company you work for take a few hints?

Remember, women who juggle their lives find that keeping all the balls in the air is exhausting . . . and exhilarating. A working mum recently exclaimed to me 'on a good day, when everything works out, you feel incredible'. And on a bad day? Well, you reach for *Juggling It All*!

CHAPTER 1

The Shape of Things to Come—Pregnancy, Maternity Leave and Your Return to Work

'Darling, I'm pregnant!' Rarely can three little words make such an impact and, hopefully, bring such joy. Of course, this announcement is not always as well received as it should be, but in the best of all possible worlds your delighted partner smothers you with kisses and breaks open the Champagne. Together you raise your glasses (yours only half full, naturally!) and contemplate the future with renewed excitement.

No wonder everyone tells you to sit down (or they do in films, anyway). Even if you were planning to start a family, your head will be spinning with more than Champagne as you try to adjust to your discovery. It's brilliant, it's wonderful . . . and slightly scary. Your life is enhanced and, as you are just beginning to realise, changed forever. Congratulations. You are now a working mother-to-be.

If you are starting a family in your early 30s as so many women now do, you have probably spent the last 10 years building up and enjoying your career. While no one can predict how you will feel once you're a mother, you anticipate returning to work at some stage after your baby is born. If you have reached a fairly senior position, that's likely to be sooner rather than later. The good news is that your life will have a new dimension; you now have the opportunity to be enriched by motherhood and family life without sacrificing your professional role.

So what's the bad news? Well, your boss might not be quite as ecstatic (particularly as you've just started work on that major project). And while some of your colleagues may react with glee, that could be because they anticipate their chance to shine in your forthcoming absence . . .

You may think that's a rather negative aspect with which to begin a chapter on pregnancy and work, when congratulations, excitement and hope seem more appropriate. But advice about when to put your feet up and making sure you get enough sleep, although important, does not address some of the underlying problems faced by working women, particularly in the tough economic climate of the 90s. Encyclopedias have been written about the effects of pregnancy on your body; until now you were unlikely to find much about the effects on your job.

As recent studies show, increasing numbers of working women return to work after maternity leave, thus continuing to give the economy the benefit of their valuable training and skills. Enlightened employers, we are told, now recognise that organising maternity cover is but a minor inconvenience in the smooth running of their companies. Well . . . that's the ideal. Sadly, many women have a very different story to tell, of covert or sometimes overt discrimination, about promotion prospects mysteriously vanishing, of colleagues staging takeover bids, of their previously secure position becoming 'redundant'.

While they're often reluctant to admit it amid all the excitement, many women suspect their hard-won respect and status will diminish during pregnancy and maternity leave, or worse, they fear their jobs are at risk. Perhaps you, newly pregnant, secretly share those feelings, particularly if you know your company is going through a lean time. All those around you seem to be tightening their belts and working longer hours, while you are expanding into elasticated waistbands and threatening to desert your post for a self-indulgent three months, possibly longer.

However, remember—forewarned is forearmed. From your hard-earned knowledge of office politics you already know that absence does *not* make the heart grow fonder. Looking forward to becoming a mother doesn't mean you have to abandon your healthy scepticism about human motivation, or ignore the basic truth that most job hierarchies, still male dominated, are highly competitive.

Help is at hand. This chapter presents a positive course of action to help you enjoy a healthy pregnancy while consolidating your position at work as far as possible. Should you need to do battle, you will find plenty of ammunition here. You will also find a plan of campaign to adopt during maternity leave which will make your working future as a mother less stressful, and will prepare you for the period of adjustment when you return to work.

Watch Your Back

Those who have a real fear they might be in danger of being sacked while away having their babies are not being paranoid. It's official. Complaints of maternity and pregnancy dismissal to the Equal Opportunities Commission have increased by 50% since January 1990. 'Having a baby? Then watch your back' warned the *Independent* newspaper. 'Women who assume that their job is safe while they are away from work on maternity leave should beware: increasing numbers are complaining of being sacked while they're off having a baby.'

For many women, fortunately, this unpleasant scenario will remain just that, as they sail through pregnancy, leave in a shower of good wishes, cuddly toys and hand-knitted bootees and are welcomed back to work by a supportive, fair-minded boss and loyal colleagues. Others will not be so fortunate, and may find themselves taken advantage of in their absence.

Pregnancy is not a time to lower your guard at work, however rosy the world looks from behind your bump. Privately, elated at your new condition, you may feel suffused with warm feeling towards your fellow humans. By all means spread a little happiness, but don't let anyone pull a fast one on you. Amazing and distracting changes will be happening to you, both physically and mentally; the future is full of possibilities. Make sure being manoeuvred out of a job isn't one of them.

For a start, most newly pregnant women find themselves at a disadvantage emotionally. Hormones can play havoc with a cool, professional exterior and your new happiness can be clouded by an unsympathetic reaction at work. If you are feeling vulnerable and coping with morning sickness, this kind of attitude can reduce the toughest nut to tears.

Even worse, while at a low point you may find yourself 'persuaded' that you won't want to come back after the birth, or that you won't be able to cope and should accept a less demanding role.

The solution is to be prepared. There are legal rights which protect you—up to an extent. But even if you *are* entitled to your job back, or full maternity pay and leave (and at time of writing, over one-third of Britain's working women didn't qualify for protection), some employers still play dirty—and get away with it.

Breaking the News

Exactly *when* to tell the boss is a dilemma faced by many women, and if handled badly, can start your pregnancy off on a sour note. Even if you've been in the same job for years, the issue is sensitive if you've recently been promoted or your department is approaching an extremely busy period. Your boss may not be the only one inconvenienced by your 'unfortunately timed' pregnancy—you may well have been taken by surprise too, and while delighted, are now faced with negotiating a major career hurdle.

Don't do anything rash

Sian Stephens is one of only 10 women to have made it to senior management level at J Sainsbury. She had just discovered she was six weeks pregnant when she was offered a rare opportunity to enter senior management.

'I was in a state of shock. When I reached 31 I started to think about trying for a baby, but it happened much sooner than I expected! Meanwhile, this promotion was something I had been working towards for 10 years since I joined the company as a graduate trainee. I suppose the job felt more real to me than the pregnancy—a feeling which was reinforced by my doctor, who said no pregnancy was regarded as viable until 12 weeks because many women miscarry before then. She told me not to do anything rash, so I took her at her word and accepted the promotion. People were ringing to congratulate me; I felt really bad. When the pregnancy was confirmed officially at 12 weeks I immediately told my director, making it very clear that I intended to return as soon as possible after the birth, although the company does operate a career break scheme. "Oh dear" was the undisguised reaction, coming seconds after genuine congratulations. However, the company was very supportive. After some discussion it was decided to put me into the post as my promotion had been announced officially. To withdraw the offer at that stage would have meant finding me another senior manager's post within the company, which come up very rarely. But I never would have accepted my promotion if I had had any doubts at all about returning quickly to the new job.'

If you anticipate problems breaking the news to your superiors, it will help if you follow the guidelines below:

● Know your basic maternity rights (they should be outlined in your contract of employment), or alternatively, contact the Maternity Alliance (see page 203) or refer to the Fact Section (see page 194).

● Be assertive—present your plans for stopping and restarting work clearly and calmly.

● Demonstrate your commitment by suggesting ways in which you can continue working during pregnancy (taking work home if necessary and changing your hours slightly, for example). Beware of having such changes made official, however, as they could affect your right to return to your old job.

Timing the announcement

When to tell your employers and colleagues is a matter for you alone to judge. Good timing is more than catching your boss in a good mood after lunch on Friday—it could be crucial to your working future. Wendy Malpass, then deputy marketing manager of the Birmingham Rep, was only a few weeks pregnant when her boss resigned. Wendy knew she could do the job well; in addition she was faced with the prospect of bringing up the baby alone after her relationship with the baby's father broke up. She desperately needed the extra money and flexibility the senior post offered, so decided to keep her pregnancy a secret when applying.

'If I didn't get the job, I knew I would have to give up working for the theatre altogether. My position as deputy involved a lot of travelling and late night work, and my existing salary was not enough for me to afford the sort of childcare I would need. I just couldn't take the risk of being honest at that stage.'

Wendy was proved right. She was appointed as marketing manager, then when she announced her pregnancy at 12 weeks was told, unofficially, that she 'wouldn't have got the job, had we known'. Wendy returned from maternity leave after three months to successfully run a busy office; she now has the financial security to enjoy both single parenthood and her career, while the theatre has not lost a valuable member of staff.

If pregnancy doesn't pose an immediate threat to your job, initial euphoria may make you feel like announcing the good news from the rooftops. But waiting a couple of weeks may make life easier all round. However, you may be found out sooner than you think!

Cheryl Armitage, now a freelance TV and radio reporter, was thoroughly enjoying her job as roving reporter for TVS when she fell pregnant. Suspecting she might be confined to the news desk, she kept the biggest story to herself.

'My husband Simon and I had been trying for four years to start a family—I was just about to start a course of IVF treatment when I became pregnant. The hospital phoned me at work with the wonderful news, and it was the hardest thing in the world for me to keep quiet. But because of my previous difficulties I didn't want to tell colleagues until I'd passed the three month mark. Also, I was due a pay increase, which I suspected I wouldn't get once they knew I was pregnant. I was also looking forward to spending an exciting weekend in Hampshire, compiling a report first hand from the back of a patrol car.

'That weekend I felt terribly sick and must have looked dreadful, because my cameraman kept asking what was wrong. I think he put it down to a couple of high speed chases, but then our car had to escort an ambulance transferring an urgent heart case to hospital. Accompanied by a film crew, we screeched into Casualty and I jumped out, shouting to the cameraman to get a close up as the ambulance doors were opened. But there, instead of the elderly chap I was expecting, was a tiny bundle in an incubator. Tears pouring down my face, I turned to the amazed crew and wailed: "It's a baby".'

That baby made a full recovery, but Cheryl's secret was out. To her surprise, after some initial teasing from the crew 'for going all mumsy' the newsroom expected her to carry on as before. Even better, her boss was genuinely pleased for her and honoured her pay rise!

Coming clean quickly

While you may not be required to spend your (concealed) pregnancy dashing about after news stories, as a general rule most doctors and psychologists recommend coming clean fairly quickly. As Cheryl's story indicates, many bosses will not respond as negatively as you fear, and they will appreciate early warning in order to organise cover. If you appear to be trying to make their job easier, you should reap the benefit.

You may need to make changes in your working pattern to

safeguard your and the baby's wellbeing. It's important that you adopt a positive, commonsense approach—you are not ill, just pregnant and you may need to make a few temporary concessions to your condition. If you feel guilty that you are not pulling your weight while pregnant, it is easy to convey this feeling to employers and colleagues.

Remember, martyred sighs and suggestions of lead swinging are just a foretaste of what's to come when you're a working mother. If you allow bossy Carruthers to make you feel bad *now* about missing one minor sales meeting for your antenatal class, she's going to make mincemeat out of you when your kid gets chicken-pox.

Be assertive about your plans for returning, should your initial announcement cause dismay. If colleagues appear to doubt your conviction, repeat your intentions to return as frequently as possible. If you hear, 'Sue is leaving us to become a mother' reply 'Yes, and I am coming back to work afterwards'. An economic argument often works best, as practically everyone can relate to 'I can't afford to give up work because of the mortgage'.

Protecting Your Health

While proving to colleagues that you can carry on as normal, beware falling into the trap of trying to be better than ever. Pregnancy is a tiring time, and you shouldn't ignore or conceal the physical and emotional changes taking place. It definitely helps to put your feet up during the day—if you haven't got a rest room at your workplace, stick your legs up on a chair and make a joke out of it to any onlookers. Counteract any embarrassment you feel by telling yourself that you'll work much better if you're not totally exhausted.

You may be concerned about the possible dangers of working with VDUs for prolonged periods during your pregnancy. No firm evidence has been produced that they can harm a foetus, but if you are worried, approach your personnel department or trade union representative. Arm yourself with the latest information by contacting City Centre (see page 203), an organisation for office workers who produce an information pack on working with VDUs.

If you find yourself struggling physically, particularly in the very early or later stages of pregnancy, be honest. Take the initiative and suggest ways in which your working hours could become more

KNOW YOUR RIGHTS

Knowing your basic rights is an important element in being assert-ive. The following gives a basic outline of statutory rights which protect pregnant women; for a detailed, step-by-step guide to retaining your job and applying for maternity pay see the Fact Section, page 194. The Maternity Alliance (see page 203) produces a useful leaflet *Pregnant at Work*.

• All pregnant women are entitled to paid time off for antenatal care, irrespective of whatever hours they work or how long they have been with the company. This can include relaxation classes, although you may need a letter from your GP, midwife or health visitor stating that such classes are part of your antenatal care.

• Pregnant women can continue to work as long as they like, even right up to labour, although most stop around 36 weeks.

• If your work is deemed hazardous or it's illegal to force you to do it during pregnancy (for example, working with X-rays or certain chemicals), or you cannot do your job adequately because of preg-nancy (for example, it involves heavy lifting), you are entitled to be moved to another job on similar terms and conditions if you have been with the same employers for:

TWO YEARS if you work full time (16 or more hours a week)
FIVE YEARS if you work part time (8–16 hours a week).

• If you have to change your work because of pregnancy and there is no suitable alternative available, only then can your employers fairly dismiss you. But you will still be entitled to paid maternity leave, provided you would have qualified for it had you not been dismissed.

• Remember that your legal right to return to your job is depen-dent on you fulfilling certain obligations to your employer, includ-ing formal notification of your intention to return. Don't rely on the personnel office to remind you, follow the detailed guide on page 196.

Good news for the future is that the EC directive on maternity rights (which becomes law in 1994) should ensure that a worker cannot be dismissed because of pregnancy. Where discrimination is alleged, the onus will not be on the employee to provide evidence as previously, but will instead rest on the employer who must con-vince a tribunal of genuine causes for dismissal. Also, pregnant women who are at present liable to be 'fairly dismissed' if their work is deemed hazardous or illegal in pregnancy will be entitled to either alternative employment or adequate financial compensation during pregnancy.

flexible, or your travelling less stressful. Could you take some work home, for example, or is there any chance of a temporary parking space in the director's car park? But be careful about allowing any temporary alteration to your hours to be written into your contract. You may find that on your return you are still bound by these restrictions. Some women have unwittingly reduced themselves to part-time status, with the resulting loss of job protection and other benefits. Keep all arrangements informal; resist pressure from colleagues and bosses, however well-meaning. Remind yourself that so long as the work still gets done, no one has valid cause for complaint.

Maternity Leave

Maternity policies vary widely between companies, as do standards of efficiency in personnel departments. Often, particularly at senior levels, arrangements for covering maternity leave can be left in the rapidly disappearing lap of the pregnant woman herself. This can be to your advantage. If you can get the blessing of your immediate boss, try to have a say in choosing your replacement, or devise an arrangement which will just be successful enough to cover your absence. (But don't be a victim of your own brilliant delegation!)

Julia, a producer for an independent television company, was invited to help choose her replacement by a wise head of department. 'I planned to turn the post into a job share, so I chose someone I felt I could work alongside when I came back to work, and trained her part time over three months. But it's very difficult having someone covering your job rather than leaving it—it's still your job yet going on without you. When I first left my replacement phoned regularly, then as her confidence grew the calls lessened and stopped, which was fine by me, as I wanted to switch off from work for a while, knowing she could handle it. She did very well, and didn't try to stage a takeover bid, which is always a possibility.' (See Chapter 11 for advice on setting up a job share and other options.)

Leave yourself enough time to train somebody, or to get new arrangements running smoothly. There's always the possibility you may go into labour earlier than expected, and you can do without panicked colleagues phoning the delivery suite. (It has been known!) Also, if your cover is haphazardly organised it may well mean you eventually return to resentment and bad feeling because the work load was not evenly spread.

But however well you plan, the actual length of time you stay away seems to be a crucial factor in how successfully you pick up the threads. Some organisations, usually in the public sector, give more generous and well-defined maternity leave, well above the statutory 29 weeks and paid at a higher rate. The rights of a maternity leave returner are clearly enshrined in the equal opportunities approved contract, which theoretically keeps the threat of office politics and hostile takeover bids to a minimum. However, this isn't always the case. If pushed to be honest, many women in senior positions working for private companies say when it comes to the crunch, exercising your rights to a lengthy maternity leave can seriously damage your job prospects.

Forcing yourself to make it all work

Sian Stephens' experience illustrates the dilemma facing women on the threshold of combining career with working motherhood. Sian was offered an important promotion to senior management with J Sainsbury just after she discovered she was pregnant. Crucial to her acceptance of her new post was her commitment to return to work as quickly as possible after the birth. She made a choice which seemed right to her, while realising the sacrifice involved.

'I had very little contact with babies before Sam was born—I had no idea what to expect but I promised to be back at work within three months. My pregnancy was trouble free and I stopped work at 38 weeks. The birth was easy, but unfortunately the baby was not! The biggest surprise was his colic, which I'd heard a little bit about. Living with it proved to be a nightmare. Sam fed every two hours until he was three months old, he had to be carried from midday until midnight. He was an enormous baby—by three months he'd reached 20 lb. I couldn't go anywhere without him, he just screamed the place down. The whole experience was immensely tiring, and when I returned to work at 14 weeks I realised I'd only been apart from him for three hours.

'During my maternity leave I tried to keep in touch with work —my deputy sent packages of information, but I got terribly behind. I didn't read a single book or newspaper, any spare moment I had I was doing Sam's washing. I never even had time to express milk for him as he fed so frequently, so I couldn't leave him with anyone for a break.'

Sian began her search for childcare early, when she was pregnant. She interviewed her shortlist of daily nannies in the four weeks before she gave birth, eventually choosing a former nursery officer who had her own nine-month-old baby.

'I did have days of terrible doubts during maternity leave. How would this little thing be able to cope without me? I was the only person who could calm him, he was so dependent. Could we survive apart? But the lives of other people were affected by my plans, I had promised to be back at work in June and the nanny gave notice to her previous job, so in a way I forced myself to make it all work.

'On my first day back at work I felt like a housewife plucked out of her home and plonked down at a desk. I kept thinking what am I doing here? Fortunately, the people around me didn't realise —I'd been away for such a short time they expected me to be just the same person. Apart from asking if I'd managed a good night's sleep, they expected my brain to be working as it was before the baby. I found that helped me regain confidence. I turned from this person with a totally dependent baby to someone back in a full-time job in the space of 24 hours. It sounds incredible, but I can't believe how well it worked. I was allowed to break myself in gently for the first week—unofficially my hours were 10–3.

'In retrospect, coming back when Sam was three months old was wonderful. I can't understand why statutory maternity leave is 29 weeks. At the time I did, even the day before I returned I did, but now I think it was best for him. I returned before he got to know me too well. Coming back after seven months would have been so selfish; he would have been so used to having me around. My only regret is that I didn't have more time with him once he'd outgrown the colic and he turned into the lovely placid baby he is now.'

While you're away

If you can stay in touch with work to some extent during your maternity leave, so much the better. But some women prefer to switch off altogether, and some have no choice as they are blessed with the kind of babies who regard mum using the phone as a gross breach of the mother and baby contract and complain bitterly the moment she gets through to the departmental manager. So much for maintaining professional esteem! No wonder many women firmly decide to switch off from work for a while.

However, having made reasonably sure about what is happening in your absence, there are various useful activities you can be pursuing to make your life easier when you return. That is, when you get time among the other delights of the most overwhelming experience of your life so far!

The early days after the birth are a totally absorbing (if not constantly enthralling) time in which your brand new job demands all your attention. You're on duty day and night and all the time there's a small, fat bald boss who never stops yelling at you. Is this what your colleagues referred to as 'taking time off'?

Once you get your head above changing mat level, there are compensations. Quite apart from the thrill of getting to know your new baby, it can be nice to live life at a different pace for a while. Many women who have spent several years dashing from home to work, morning and night, discover the delights of the local community, like having time to chat up the local butcher and getting to know your neighbours. It's also very useful—the value to the working mother of a local support network cannot be underestimated.

Christine Davis and Catherine Tutton, co-directors of the Return Consultancy, specialise in all aspects of women returning to work. Their long experience of counselling and advising working mothers, including those pregnant or on maternity leave, has given them valuable insight. As part of one of their in-house workshops, *The Positive Approach to Pregnancy, Motherhood and Return to Work*, Chris and Catherine recommend a plan of action to be undertaken during maternity leave. Even though you intend to return to work full time, use some of your brief sojourn at home to become more involved in the community:

● Get to know other new mothers locally; you may think it pointless if you are going back to work, but it's worth making the effort to keep up the friendships, even on an irregular basis after your return. Stay-at-home mums especially, if you don't exploit them, can provide useful back-up help if childcare arrangements fail. It's important to keep your side of the bargain—possibly repaying with evening/weekend babysitting.

● Start making connections at your antenatal class; you'll all be going through the same stages at roughly the same time. Or attend a local postnatal mother and baby exercise class—stretching and toning (or retching and groaning, as it comes to be known!) is a great way of cementing friendships. Going out to a regular class with your baby forces you to get back into a routine and you'll feel much better when you see other new mothers making the same mistakes as you.

• Now is the time to start organising childcare. Detailed information on all choices is in the following chapters, but the golden rule is whatever your choice, leave yourself plenty of time to make arrangements. Remember that you will need time to settle your child in before you return to work.

• Grab a Granny! In these days of scattered families, you may not have your own mother close at hand to help out. Getting to know older women (who like children!) can be to your mutual benefit, particularly if they are willing to help out with emergency childminding, housesitting etc. A physically robust and with-it 'Granny' might also be willing to enter into a more regular arrangement with school age children, who need picking up and minding for just a couple of hours a day before you get home from work.

• Maternity leave is also a time for taking a long, cool look at what it's going to cost you to return to work. The cost factor will probably predetermine your choice of childcare, of course, but there are many other expenses which shouldn't be overlooked. Don't underestimate—the cost of going out to work with a small child is *very high*. Out of your net income, you need to subtract:

1 Cost of childcare
2 Fares or petrol to and from work, plus any to and from childminder or nursery
3 Cost of convenience foods for the baby and your family (if you would cook your own at home)
4 Cost of disposable nappies (if you would use terries if you stayed home)
5 Your lunches at work
6 Extra expense of smarter work clothes if you work in an office
7 Cost of a cleaner (*not* a luxury, say many working mothers)
8 Unavoidable work expenses, leaving presents, birthday lunches, rounds at the pub, union subscriptions etc.

Returning to Work

How lovely to be welcomed with open arms, by selfless colleagues who have spent the past six months doing their job plus the boring bits of yours, or be welcomed by a graciously smiling deputy who quietly slips out of your desk and back into obscurity behind the partition. How lovely . . . and frankly, how unlikely.

Unfortunately, women who return from maternity leave may find their job has been given to someone else and they are often in a difficult position to fight back. An employer is within his or her legal rights to offer a job of equivalent status and pay, even if it's in another department or even at another location. It is always worth tackling the personnel or equal opportunities officer, however, particularly if your firm prides itself on go-ahead policies which aren't being put into practice.

However, the issues may be less clear cut. You may return from maternity leave to find that the most enjoyable and responsible parts of your job have been creamed off by a rival who is now most unwilling to give them back. Or you may discover that you have been passed over for promotion, which is what happened to Elaine, a museum programme co-ordinator who returned from her second maternity leave to find that a junior male rival had been promoted permanently at her expense. Furious at apparent collusion between male 'buddies', she decided to fight fire with fire.

'While I was off on maternity leave I kept in touch and was fully aware that this man was being "temporarily" promoted in my absence. But it was clear when I returned that he was going to stay put and no one was prepared to challenge him. At first I felt pain, rather than anger; I was hurt that my boss, with whom I had worked for several years, could have let this happen. I couldn't take it any higher officially, as a new director had been appointed during my maternity leave and I was reluctant to start off on the wrong foot with him. After six months in the cosy world of children I'd lost the edge you need to fight.'

However, after a couple of days feeling upset, Elaine began to get mad. She realised there was another, more subtle way to bring her case to the director's attention. 'I used a network—just like a man would. I realised that the new director and I had a mutual friend, someone who was a really good pal of mine. So I went to see him and burst into tears (quite genuinely). He was astonished and promised to let my director know, informally, what had been going on.'

When the director called Elaine in, he said he was furious that no one in the personnel department had told him about the case. While he blustered, Elaine was able to appear as the sweet voice of reason. 'I told him calmly that although I was most unhappy about it, I didn't want to name names and cause a fuss about unfair employment practices when he had only just started in the job!'

Elaine's coolness paid dividends—she was offered an alternative promotion, leading her into more creative work which she enjoys. 'I even got an apology from my boss—albeit a mumbled "sorry" when we both happened to be waiting by the photocopier one day!'

Discrimination against maternity leave returners is a new area of law, with few precedents. The Equal Opportunities Commission (EOC) can help women fight cases at Industrial Tribunal, but only

---

WHAT TO DO IF YOU'RE FIRED

Have you been with the same employer for TWO YEARS full time or FIVE YEARS part time?
You can take your employer to an Industrial Tribunal for unfair dismissal under the Employment Protection Act.
Have you been with this employer for less than TWO years full time or FIVE part time?
You can take action under the Sex Discrimination Act.

The first step is to get *legal advice* to determine whether your case is worth pursuing—and the likely cost. Legal aid is not available for Industrial Tribunals. You must take action within three months.
Contact:
• your trade union representative
• a solicitor
• The Maternity Alliance
• The Equal Opportunities Commission (EOC), though they will only financially back those who are likely to set a legal precedent.

If you are determined to fight a so-called 'redundancy', hold your ground. Beware of being persuaded to resign under pressure, as you will forgo any right to compensation.

Sometimes the threat of an Industrial Tribunal will cause employers to settle out of court to avoid adverse publicity.

Remember that the maximum an Industrial Tribunal can award is £10,000, and your employer is not obliged to take you back. It may be worth conserving your energies to negotiate with your guilty employer for the best possible 'golden handshake' you can get.

if they feel they will win and be able to establish new precedents in this grey area. If you feel you have been unfairly treated, but are not sure if it could be classed as sexual discrimination, contact the EOC at the address on page 203. They don't pretend taking your employers to tribunal is a quick, easy process, but by fighting now you could also be helping other working mothers in the future.

Combining work and motherhood

Of course, you may experience no unpleasantness, but it's as well to be prepared. Expect the worst, and you may be pleasantly surprised. But there may be those who don't understand about the hard work of having a baby and looking after it and think you've spent months swanning around enjoying yourself. Or worse, those who just aren't interested (or pretend they're not) in hearing even the barest details of your major achievement. This can be hurtful. Even if you weren't planning a daily bulletin on your offspring's amazing progress, it's perfectly natural to want some acknowledgement.

You shouldn't be expected to slot back into work as if nothing had happened and indeed, for the sake of all working mothers, you shouldn't try. It will take courage, but if you are being unfairly treated or experiencing problems with a new routine, you must speak up. Playing at Superwoman because you're too proud to admit what a struggle you're having will increase your stress, and it won't help other women seek help, if they fear being compared to such a paragon. Combining work and motherhood successfully is a major juggling act, and the responsibilities of a working mother must not be understated.

Chris Davis and Catherine Tutton of the Return Consultancy have hijacked the concept of 'outing', which they recommend to those attending their pre-maternity workshops. A milder variation based on the public exposure of homosexuals, they urge experienced working mothers, particularly those in visible high-status positions, to come clean about the problems they may have encountered at work, and to stop pretending that they have never agonised about leaving their children.

However, the major responsibility rests with the employers, who must realise that the experience of pregnancy and return to work is a massive life change, analogous with the impact of retirement and that they can prepare their employees. As Chris says:

'Many employers now recognise the value of providing pre-retirement courses for their predominantly male employees to help them adjust to the massive life change that retirement brings. Yet the other massive life change that working women experience, the adjustment to motherhood and how to combine home and work, is only just beginning to be addressed seriously by a minority of employers. We aim to make our pre-maternity leave workshops for women as accepted by organisations as the pre-retirement courses are now.'

On the immediate practical front, there are several tips which Chris and Catherine recommend if you are finding the first few weeks or months very hard:

- Stick it out—if you feel you can't cope with being back at work tell yourself, not your employer, that you will give it three months (or whatever). If you still feel you've made a mistake, at least you've given yourself time to be really sure.
- Resist all attempts by a well-meaning or misguided boss to 'ease the strain' of your job by giving all the exciting and interesting parts to someone else while you settle in. Apart from the real risk you may never get them back, a mundane job can be equally stressful, and it is extremely galling when you've got all keyed up for your return.
- If you think changes to your working hours might help, suggest a range of solutions rather than an all or nothing proposition. Diplomacy is the key.
- Be aware that there is still a great deal of prejudice against job share or part-time working—you will have to be determined.
- Express your delight and appreciation when management makes a positive move to help—like children they need a lot of encouragement!
- There's strength in numbers—start up a Working Parents Group within your organisation (see below).

A problem shared

'You are not alone' is an encouraging thought, but how do you meet other working mothers within a large organisation, particularly one based in a huge impersonal building? Starting up a Working Mothers (or Parents if you prefer) Group is one way to get them to come to you. You could begin with the personnel department and ask for details of those who qualify (you might like to

include those women who are pregnant, too). If there is a staff
newsletter, you could place an announcement, or circulate a memo.
If you prefer a low-key, unofficial approach, try a discreet mention
of an out-of-hours meeting of mums.

The Boots Working Mothers Group, based in Nottingham, was
initiated by Anne Toler, Personnel Manager for Central Services.
She had returned to work after the birth of her first child, Claire,
and wanted to share her experiences with other working mums.
The group began as an informal, unofficial meeting during a
lunchhour, and about 20 mums attended. 'We didn't just dwell on
problems,' remembers Anne. 'It was nice just to talk over all the
issues with women who understood.'

As support grew, Anne approached management for official
backing in what was really a *fait accompli*. She made it clear the
group was not seeking confrontation over maternity issues, but
wished to be a positive force for change. The group, which meets
five or six times a year, now numbers around 100 mums who work
at the Boots headquarters. Once newly pregnant women inform
the personnel office they are invited to come along to meetings,
where they can seek help and encouragement to come back to work
after the birth. The group offers three basic services:
• A list of home addresses and phone numbers of all members,
plus local childcare information
• The chance to hear outside speakers on a variety of subjects
• A quarterly newsletter produced and written by members

As a group, Boots working mothers have achieved several positive steps forward. Working mothers in each division of Boots were
asked to write to their individual personnel managers suggesting
how the company could help with their childcare needs. This has
led to the company subsidising places at local nurseries. A need
was also identified for holiday playschemes to help the parents of
school age children, which led to a new Boots-sponsored scheme
being run for five–14 year olds over the summer. And one small but
useful gain—the Working Mothers Group campaigned successfully
for Boots' staff discount to be extended to cover women on
maternity leave.

More recently a Working Parents Group has been set up with
Shell UK by Ann Martin-Herbert, a senior technical advisor. She
returned to work after having Theo, now two, and after receiving
the official go-ahead contacted other working mothers through
noticeboard announcements. The group meets monthly during a

lunchhour to hear visiting speakers or for a discussion meeting, when members can air common problems and learn how colleagues are coping. With proof of genuine interest and need from WPG members, Ann was able to persuade management to invite the Return Consultancy to run several in-house workshops for women on maternity leave and those just back at work, which have proved very successful.

CHAPTER 2

How to Enjoy it All (without feeling too guilty!)

'There is no happier creature alive than a working mother who is firing well on all cylinders. Believe me, I've been one, sometimes for whole weeks at a time,' says Madeleine Kingsley, writing in *SHE* about those glorious stretches when everything is going well at work and at home and you feel you could conquer the world. But she acknowledges the down side too.

'There are grim times, when you are run ragged by the conflicting claims of work and home, and, like wartime margarine, you feel as if you're spread too thinly to linger fulfillingly over any task long enough to pause and enjoy it.' These are the times when every working mother will ask herself 'is it really worth it?'

'The short answer is, and must remain, *yes*,' counsels Madeleine, busy journalist and mother of three. 'Yes, despite the guilty frustration and frazzle, it certainly is worth working—even if it's for just a few hours a week—to give yourself the threefold advantages of confidence, independence and outside interest. It is worth working because, as the children grow older, your fatigue will lessen and your capacity to do the best for them in terms of good shoes, music lessons and generally seeing the world will increase. It is worth working to avoid having all your eggs of fulfilment in one precarious basket.'

Joy and Pain

It's important to remind yourself of the reasons you have chosen the challenge of combining work and motherhood—particularly as a defence against those prophets of doom and despondency who liken working motherhood to a treadmill of stress, guilt and exhaustion. As those fortunate to have a choice, let's acknowledge the sheer joy of combining a fulfilling paid job with raising a family. Of course there are immense practical and emotional problems to face along the way, but you persevere because it's marvellous to feel you have an identity, not just a role, and to realise how much richer your life has become.

However, in order to realise this investment, you may need to develop a few survival tactics for when the going gets rough. Guilt serves as a useful warning device for any mother and should not be ignored, but working mothers are especially vulnerable and have to fight harder to keep the destructive old devil firmly in check. Be prepared to fight; you will never win the war, but need never lose the battle!

This chapter suggests some useful strategies for coping emotionally with the juggling act, and offers the thoughts of many experienced working mothers who, by coming to terms with rather than suppressing their doubts and anxieties, allow themselves to enjoy their busy and rewarding lives.

An inspiring example is former secretary Janice, who has retrained as an accountant, does the books for her husband's self-employed business, and pursues a rigorous study schedule as well as coping with her two children of 11 and nine. She describes herself as 'resourceful and tenacious', having pulled her life back together after losing everything when her first marriage failed. However, she still has to keep her guilt in check.

'I sometimes feel that because I do so much I don't do anything to the best of my ability; that I spread myself too thinly between husband, children and work. To combat this I have rationalised my guilt and accepted the situation—in fact, I have let myself off the hook! After all, guilt is such a terrible waste of energy.'

Julie Lock, company PA and mother of two, admits that she has never learnt to cope with the occasional tearful goodbye at the nursery, but never expects to. She does not let this stop her expressing pride in what she has achieved.

'I have a good job and I know I am highly thought of at work, as well as being a good mother with two fantastic kids. I cope with work, children, finances and running the home alone with no help from my husband, who is presently unemployed. I'm capable in my own right, and that makes me feel strong and proud.'

Acknowledge How You Feel

While being relaxed about the housework will give you more time to enjoy your family, it's futile to sweep the emotional problems under the carpet. If you are plagued by demons of doubt and guilt, shake them out into the light. Talking about how you feel helps tremendously, particularly with other working mothers, who are unlikely to dismiss your feelings as insignificant. Taking the wider perspective, 'owning up' also helps chip away at the oppressive Superwoman myth and makes it easier for women to help one another, particularly at senior levels within organisations.

On a more intimate level, if you have a sympathetic partner, that's a major plus, of course. But many men find it hard to understand this dilemma—they have always been encouraged to want and expect to combine both family and work. While they may well applaud your decision to go back to work they may be bemused at the conflicting emotions you feel, as described by social worker Angela MacDonald.

'After having my second child I did feel very bored at home and couldn't wait to get back to work. *That* made me feel a bit guilty. But I really enjoy my independence and the financial and emotional reward of having a career, and having a life outside the home where you can be yourself (something men have always enjoyed without a second thought).'

By not underestimating the powerful emotions that may pull you different ways (and realising you are *not* the only one who ever agonised!), you can develop a more successful defence. For example, quite apart from the other hurdles of returning to work, leaving a baby or young child for the first time is unbelievably painful for many women, and can take a new working mother completely unawares.

Gil Evans, a senior educational psychologist and mother of four, believes that those leaving pangs affect us far more than we think. Gil runs informal workshops for working mothers finding it hard to cope emotionally, and she says: 'Your best preparation is to acknowledge that guilt is unavoidable. Providing you've got a good carer, trust her. And remember that however tough it is initially to return to work, both you and your children will soon learn to adjust.'

Look at the Evidence!

There are plenty of hard facts to back this up, including those contained in the findings of the Day Care Project, a major survey carried out by the Thomas Coram Research Unit in London. This six-year study looked at the difference a first baby made to the careers of both mother and father, together with the effects that the necessary full time childcare had on the children.

Many of the women returners in the study said they felt bereft at leaving their babies, and described a sense of real physical loss. But most surprised themselves by recovering, often within a week of being back in the office, an experience shared by Further Education lecturer Susan Robertson from Chester.

'When I first left Andrew at 3½ months I was heartbroken, but after a few weeks I settled down and so did he. I'd say give your work a real chance, choose the right person to look after your child, and *relax*. I'm no Superwoman, I'm just ordinary and anyone can do it if I can. The worst time for me was when Andrew had disturbed nights. My husband is the world's worst getter-upper so it was all down to me. I was tired and resentful, but I managed. I seemed to draw on other strengths and learned to only do essential things. If you feel guilty about not doing everything you'll go under.'

Research officer Sue Martin, a psychologist who directed the childcare side of the study, produced immensely reassuring evidence about the effects of childcare. Sue's team looked at 250 children from different backgrounds who were variously cared for by parents, relatives, childminders and private day nurseries. Their social, emotional, cognitive and language development were assessed at four and 18 months, and again at three and six years.

Researchers found there was *no difference* between the children whose mothers worked and those who were at home, at any stage, except at 18 months and three years when those children in day nurseries showed greater social competence, although displaying slightly less advanced language skills. This difference, however, had disappeared by the time children had reached six, and all were at school.

Expecting to find differences in psychological wellbeing at least, Sue carried out a further special study of 30 children at home and 30 in day nurseries which again failed to discover any variations. 'My view,' says Sue confidently, 'is that women should work if they want to—with good quality daycare their children will not suffer.'

Facing the Critics

It's useful to arm yourself mentally with such knowledge as a defence against surprise attack. Quoting statistics will not silence a critic, but you can use them as a private mantra to keep your blood pressure down! The personal intimidation from some of your 'nearest and dearest' can be hard to counter. It's probably best to save your breath. Sandra Scarr and Judy Dunn make the following wry comment in their book *MotherCare/Othercare* published by Penguin in 1987:

'The major problem of relatives' and friends' disapproval of your working is that you know you will be blamed for anything which goes wrong with your child. If he has problems of any kind—social, emotional, intellectual or physical—you will be responsible for not having provided a proper home. Everything from shyness to ingrowing toenails will be attributable to you working, not to mention major mental illness or retardation. If he does well, he will have succeeded *despite* your neglect. If your child turns out to be a star, don't count on accolades for a job well done.'

Keeping a tight grip on your sense of humour really helps to keep everything in proportion. Barbara, a dyslexia teacher from south Wales, calls her local branch of the mother's mafia 'the tafia' after being on the receiving end of a few sharp comments about working mothers. However, Barbara feels lucky to get off so lightly. Her boss was one of the first women to return from maternity leave back in the mid-70s and had to cope with a barrage of negative attitudes. One disapproving colleague actually ignored her for *six years*!

Be prepared for less overt criticism, too. Helen Wiseman, an Access Centre administrator at Norwich College of Further Education, is always on her guard when dealing with health practitioners.

'If I take a sick child to the doctors I am invariably asked if I work. Health visitors especially have a knack of inducing guilt if your child is under five. I usually respond by saying they have fantastic professional and loving care.'

Another powerful argument for the defence is that a happy mother makes happy children. There are those who delight in and will excel at full-time mothering, but a depressed woman at home with children who longs to work does not make a good mother—

in fact, evidence suggests that her lack of responsiveness and interest will eventually damage the emotional development of her child.

Sue, a senior reporter on a Welsh weekly newspaper, suffered
severe postnatal depression after the birth of her second child,
starting when he was eight months old. 'Counselling helped me
realise that I just wasn't suited to being a stay-at-home mother,
even though I was doing a part-time job as well. I finally overcame
my guilt complex about full-time working and enrolled on a journ-
alism course at 36—I was their oldest ever student! I have never
suffered depression since, and I am told I am much easier to live
with. It's lovely having your mind stretched creatively at work *and*
having the cosiness of family life.'

A move in the opposite direction, from full- to part-time work,
helped Gillian Powell feel good about doing both. A former PR
Officer for the Metropolitan Police and now working as a freelance
newspaper journalist in Somerset, Gillian describes how she felt
when she tried full-time motherhood after the birth of her daughter
Daisy, now three: 'Part of me withered. I function much better as
a parent when I have the stimulus and satisfaction of work.' However, she decided to reduce her hours in order to combine the two.

'I feel I am lucky to have interesting work and the rewards and
benefits (which I never expected) of motherhood. My career may
be on ice, but that is a small sacrifice for a life which is full in a
new way. Moving from a demanding career to part-time work is
good practice for retirement—without work or family, life could
be meaningless for a 60-year-old female workaholic.'

Elizabeth Higgins, a health contracts manager for Waltham
Forest Health Authority in East London, negotiated a job share in
order to see more of her two children, Angus, two and a half, and
Amelia, seven months: 'I now work part time because I know that
I would feel guilty if I continued full time. I can enjoy the balance
between practical caring roles at home and mental stimulation and
productivity at work.'

Older and Wiser

Many working mothers who found making the transition from
home to work fairly painless when they had tiny babies find it gets
more difficult as those children get older. Marion, a part-time and
freelance picture researcher from Essex, admits that while she finds

juggling work and motherhood a positive challenge ('I've always enjoyed a busy life!'), she increasingly misses her daughter Amy who is two and a half. 'I enjoy her company more now she's older and I often wonder what she's doing during the day.'

In addition to your children becoming 'more interesting' as they grow older, they are also more able to articulate their discontent at your working. While you can silence screams and wails with cuddles and food, a child who can talk is less easily comforted. Needless to say, this is when the guilt reactor really blows a fuse, as Alison, a marketing executive and mother of Rosy, three, has discovered: 'Rosy frequently asks if she can stay home from nursery. I combat this by saying that sometimes I don't like to go to work either. But she has just asked me if I found looking after her boring, and was that why I went to work!'

Patricia, a solicitor, is experiencing problems now her son is at school. 'Aged five, he has recently become very expansive on the subject of other children's mothers picking them up from school. But I personally feel more guilty in admitting that I enjoy my children far more if I've had some time away from them.'

It does get better when they get older, but only if you adopt the right attitude, thinks Susan Beddoes, who works with homeless ex-offenders and has two children of 16 and ten. After bringing them up alone she now feels the guilt is lessening: 'I do suffer a bit, but not as much as I used to. I know guilt is negative, so I try not to take it on board. Children are not our property; we have the job of raising them and equipping them to live independent and successful lives. I consider I am doing that, so why feel guilty? It is so nice now when we all come together at the end of the day —I appreciate my children far more since I started working.'

Making Time to Talk

Judy Walder, whose two oldest daughters are 21 and 18, still experiences guilt when her youngest daughter (13) wishes mum could be there to greet her after school. 'I miss that too,' admits Judy, who works as a product development technologist. 'But I recognise we won't always feel like this. I always make sure we have time to go over her day together later.' Judy is well aware of the importance of her work now her family is nearly grown up. 'I really enjoy being my own person with a busy life outside the home. Having a job means I am not living too much through my daughters' lives.'

While older children demand less physical attention, they need more emotional support, and fitting in time for heart-to-hearts is not easy in a busy household. But beware trying to initiate a flood of confidences to release your own feelings.

'Guilt can make you overpowering,' warns Tim Kahn of Parent Network, an organisation which provides education and support for parents to help them get on better with their children. 'Scheduling "time to talk" may satisfy your need to feel like a good parent, but it won't necessarily mean you communicate with your child. Not all children want to talk at a regular time; some will unload at bedtime, others prefer to tackle things over low-key activities like the washing up. If you set things up you are doomed for disappointment. It's better to make yourself available. Don't interrogate—if you suspect something has happened at school, for example, then you could try describing the problems of *your* day, as this sometimes gets a response.'

Parent Network administers advice and help through local groups, which are led by specially trained parents who have been helped by the Network themselves. The specific problems encountered by working mothers are often addressed within these groups, and Tim feels that the Network has a lot to offer.

'We help people realise that they can learn how to be "good enough" parents—the perfect parent just doesn't exist. We try to provide practical suggestions to help deal with guilt. One working mother complained that she was pounced on by the kids the moment she came through the door at night and found it impossible to deal with all the problems, arguments and requests. This made her feel guilty and unhappy. We suggested a compromise— the children would make her a cup of tea and leave her alone for ten minutes to recuperate before she attended to them.'

Down With Quality Time—On With Quality Life!

It's time to sling out one of the most over-used, guilt inducing slogans of working motherhood. The tacky cliché 'quality time' gets the guilt monitors buzzing in all the working mothers I know —we are all subconsciously measuring our out-of-work hours against some improbable notion, which goads us (if we let it) into fretting that the fun we have with our children is not as deeply meaningful as the fun they're giving theirs next door.

In the questionnaires sent out to research this book, I asked if working mothers put aside any time 'exclusively' for their children. Inferring a value judgement, similar shame-faced replies came back time and time again: 'It's not what you would call "quality time", we just have a story and a cuddle . . .' 'Usually I'm too tired and irritable, but we make bathtime fun' . . . 'My biggest worry is lack of "quality time" with the boys—I always seem to be doing something else with them.' Julie Lock summed it up for many with her honest appraisal of how she felt she failed to match up to some imaginary ideal: 'After a hard day at work it takes genuine will-power to set aside a period of time for the kids because one is continually guilty about housework, husband etc. There is also an overwhelming urge to collapse in front of the TV . . . I listen to my children read every night at bedtime and we also make the most of bathtime. Sundays are also sometimes a special day for us. However, with all the other things requiring my attention sometimes it is hard to devote as much time to them as I would like.'

Being a working mother does telescope some of the experience of parenthood. Physically you have less time with your children and naturally you want to make the most of your time together. The notion of quality time—a sort of meaningful 'cramming' session—is so narrow a definition of this shared time that it spoils the pleasure of just simply being together, doing silly little things, cuddling in front of the television, everyday events which express your love and let your child feel secure and happy.

A better way to enjoy these precious moments is to accept the limitations of working motherhood and make the most of shared time together, rather than trying to squeeze eight hours of full-time mothering into a 45-minute bath and bedtime routine. Unfortunately, no British institute has felt this subject worthy of study as yet, but American research has looked at the way employment alters a woman's maternal style without her being aware of it, changes the rules of attachment (the bond between mother and child) and speeds up the development timetable for the first four years of a child's life.

In his fascinating and strangely moving book *The Woman Who Works, The Parent Who Cares* (Bantam Press, 1988), Dr Sirgay Sanger explains his work with a group of American working mothers and the development of a new style of 'Reality Attuned

Parenting' (REAP) which meets the challenges of combining work and family. In a splendidly eloquent and American way, Dr Sanger (who dedicates his work to 'the heroines of the twentieth century') provides a massive and much needed morale boost for working mothers everywhere: '. . . a dozen recent studies show the working mother's infant or toddler as more socially skilled, emotionally mature, self sufficient, intellectually adventurous and independent than children whose mothers don't work. Without quite intending it, then, you and other working women have done something at once audacious and deeply validating. You have raised a new kind of child: one who displays strengths not usually seen in the first four years of life and who possesses values that suggest that Western society in the twenty-first century will be a more understanding, open, tolerant—better—place to live.'

Remember that next time someone calls you selfish.

CHAPTER 3

Choosing Your Childcare

In this chapter you will find an at-a-glance guide to the various types of childcare available, how to find them and what they will cost at 1992 prices, in and outside London. The various options are explored more fully (in all their emotional and practical complexity!) in following chapters.

Good quality, reliable childcare is undeniably the most important factor contributing to a working mother's success and happiness; the firm basis on which she can continue to perform her precarious daily juggling of work and family commitments. But unlike her European sisters, a British woman can expect little help in finding and paying for this crucial resource. While the government insists the economy needs her skills, it still maintains that provision of childcare is a private, not public responsibility. As Malcolm Wicks, Director of the Family Policy Studies Centre, observed at a *SHE* conference on the family: 'Compared with many of our successful European partners who have seen both the economic and social sense of childcare, our position has been one of shameful neglect.'

This situation must, and will change. Powerful voices are lobbying on behalf of the family, and governments will have to listen. The future looks promising, but in the meantime, you, working mother elect, have to sort out something before the end of your maternity leave.

The golden rule when you embark on the search is to give yourself plenty of time. Be persistent, even tenacious, when dealing with local authority departments. Explore all the options available in your area, and talk to as many other mothers as possible in order to make a considered, well-informed choice, so far as a choice exists.

A realistic approach is to decide what you can afford and what are your essential requirements, then see what is available in your area. Hopefully you will be able to achieve a balance between all three which doesn't compromise your principles. It can be tempting, particularly when demand outstrips supply, to grab the first carer who seems pleasant, without considering the practicalities. You might be extremely lucky, or you may find yourself altering your entire weekly routine to fit in with the unforeseen inflexibility of a childminder's hours or the horrendous journey to and from a nursery.

Don't despair, however difficult it may seem at the outset. Think creatively around the problem. If you leave yourself plenty of time, perhaps even starting to look while you are pregnant, you can get your name down on waiting lists and explore as many options as possible. Tell as many people as you can think of that you are looking for childcare: just chatting to friends and neighbours may lead some of them to offer their services as minders (remember they will need to register with the Social Services).

Before You Start Looking

Before you start the search for suitable childcare, first sit down in a quiet moment and consider what you want for your child and yourself.

● Do you want your child to be cared for in an exclusive one-to-one relationship, as with a nanny, or nanny share, or in a group situation of a nursery, or to a lesser extent, a childminder?

● Would you prefer an element of creative stimulation and learning activities or is a cosy, family atmosphere with more cuddles and affection most important?

● Do you want continuity of care from your return to work until your child is at school? A nanny is unlikely to provide this, a childminder more so. A childminder will often be willing to take your child to and from part-time nursery school, and some will continue to escort and pick up children to and from school. The majority of private day nurseries, although providing reliable full-time care, will only take children over two.

● What can you afford? It's important to work out exactly what childcare will swallow up out of your net salary each month. You may find that after all the other working expenses are deducted you are left with less money in your pocket than your carer. This bizarre situation, which can last until your child is at school, is acceptable to some mothers who choose to go out to work for the other benefits (and whose employed partners acquiesce in their plans—an important plus).

• Do you need flexibility? If your job frequently demands that you stay late or arrive early, you will quickly fall out with a child-minder, and nursery hours may be too rigid. Perhaps a nanny or nanny share would be a better choice.

• Are you prepared to travel to a minder's house or nursery (with all equipment, spare clothes etc. in all weathers)? Or are you so bad at organising yourself in the mornings that you would prefer someone to pick up from or come to your house?

• Will it be very difficult to take time off for your child's illness? If you use a childminder or nursery you're more prone to problems

---

WHAT WILL IT COST?

The figures below (compiled in 1992) should be taken as a rough guide; pay and fees tend to vary from area to area, rather than obeying a strict divide between London and the rest of the country. For example, a Bristol childminder living near the University and looking after a lecturer's children can charge a rate equivalent to London, while a few miles away in the area of St Paul's she'd be lucky to earn the NCMA recommended minimum of £55 a week. Private day nursery fees *are* lower in the north, where qualified nursery nurses earn as little as £4000 a year. After-school clubs and holiday playschemes are all subsidised to a greater or lesser extent and are fairly similar. Bear in mind that childminders are working mothers too, and deserve fair pay; if you are employing a nanny or mother's help it will pay you in the long run to be as generous as you can afford.

Type of care	*Net cost per week (full time)*
Childminder	£55–85
Nanny (live in) (qualified and experienced)	£80–125 (plus food and lodging)
Nanny (live out) (qualified and experienced)	£150–£200
Nanny Share	£200–£250 (depending on the number of children)
Mother's Help (experienced but not qualified)	£80–100
Au Pair	£30–35 pocket money
Private Day Nursery	£75–145
After-school Club	£15
Holiday Playscheme	£50

—neither will take more than a mildly ill child. A childminder's own illness, or that of her children, will mean you lose days. And bear in mind that bugs spread like wildfire in a nursery!

Childcare Options: Pros and Cons

Below is a guide to the various types of childcare available, and the pros and cons you should consider.

Relatives

Naturally the loving care offered by a known and trusted relative (particularly granny) would be most working mothers' first choice. But there are a few pros and cons to consider before handing over junior to a beaming mum-in-law or cooing cousin.

Pros

- Inexpensive (and some relatives wouldn't dream of accepting money).

- You know and love their funny little ways.

- A familiar and trusted figure for the child, who will provide sense of continuity and a normal family life.
- May be very flexible about hours.
- Probably more willing to cope with illness which other carers would not accept.

- No need for a close relative to register as a childminder.

- No bureaucracy, contract or administration to deal with.

Cons

- Will you be able to repay them in some other way, or will you always uncomfortably be in their debt?
- Ideas on child-rearing differ widely between generations—can you bear it when *your* Mum 'knows best'?
- An informal arrangement can end without formal notice.

- May feel free to have a good old nag if you are late from work.
- The older the relative the more prone they are to illness. Also they may underestimate the energy needed to deal with a lively toddler all day.
- Informal nature of the relationship can lead to exploitation, or at least suspicion of it. Resentment can build up quickly.

Childminder (see also Chapter 4)

Child is looked after by formally unqualified, but Social Services approved person, in her own home. She's usually a mum, and will combine looking after her children with others. (No more than six under-eights/three under-fives, including hers.) Hours are usually 8 am–6 pm, although some minders will have children overnight or unusual hours for shift workers. Children fit in with normal daily activities of a household, shopping, playing, outings. Education is informal and close to what you would probably provide yourself. The best minders have plenty of stimulating toys and activities to offer.

How to find one
Your local Social Service department will have a list of registered minders and vacancies (some are better organised than others).
• Some minders prefer to advertise in local shop windows. (Always check they are registered.) Or try advertising there yourself.
• Set up your own arrangement, you may find someone ideal, except that she is not registered. She should contact Social Services promptly, as the bureaucracy and 'vetting' procedures take time.
• The National Childminding Association may be able to help by putting you in touch with a local minders' group.
• Your local branch of the Working Mothers Association may have useful advice based on the experience of other mums.

Pros
• Relatively cheap.
• Friendly, homely atmosphere.

• Your child can enjoy the company of others.
• Good support network, i.e. the NCMA who encourage use of local toy libraries etc.
• A committed minder can provide care up to school age and then part time, beyond that.

Cons
• Cost doubles for siblings.
• Care rather than formal education, but plenty of stimulation.
• More possibility of infection.

• As a private individual with her own family, a minder is vulnerable to other pressures, e.g. her husband's redundancy or job move. Also, older children will probably need the stimulation of part-time nursery school from three upwards. This means your choice will be limited to a nursery near your childminder.

• Care out of your house which saves on heating, lighting etc. and you can leave it looking like a tip.

• Have all hassle of travel, with buggies, carrycots etc. and the early morning rush involved.

• The illness problem—an ill child cannot go to the minder's and an ill minder, or one with her own ill children, cannot be expected to mind. However, some have back-up arrangements with other local NCMA minders.

Nannies (see also Chapter 5)

Your child is looked after by a qualified and/or experienced person in your own home. Nannies will do child-related housework; their meals, laundry, cleaning etc. You pay for qualifications but they should be able to have sole charge of children immediately. Can live in (possibly home at weekends) or come daily.

How to find one
• Word of mouth. Do not underestimate the power of the so-called nanny grapevine. Its main purpose is to spread juicy gossip about employers, but it can be used to spread the word that you are looking. Ask a friend with a nanny to mention it to her, and wait for results!
• Advertising. Locally: try a card in a newsagent's window or, much more effective, a popular children's toy or clothes shop. A local paper will spread the word further. Nationally: the two stalwarts are *The Lady* and *Nursery World*.
• Agencies. These will charge what seems to be a steep fee but may save time and trouble in the long run.
• Approaching schools and colleges direct for newly qualified nannies. Don't forget this includes local colleges of further education which run NNEB courses. Or try your local jobcentre, or even Careers Office as an outside chance.

Pros
• Takes over the morning rush, so you can waltz out, unencumbered, and go straight to work.

Cons
• A live-out nanny can leave without much notice. Live-outs rarely stay longer than a year, so continuity can be a problem.

• Flexible. Much more conducive to working late/early if you need it.

• One-to-one relationship (depending on number of children you have).

• Children can be rather isolated unless nanny gets out and about.

• A good nanny, free from housework, will educate and stimulate your children with creative activities, messy play etc.

• In theory you have more control over care than with minder or nursery.

• You may need to pay for a cleaner to cope with housework.

• In reality there is a lack of supervision—a bad nanny can get up to no good.

• The onus for vetting is totally on you.

• Can provide chauffeur service for children, providing transport is available.

• Someone at home to deter burglars, let in plumbers etc.

• Higher insurance premiums if nanny borrows your car; some demand use of car on days off.

• More wear and tear, higher food and fuel bills (especially with live-in nanny).

• Live-in available for regular babysitting.

• Loss of privacy/space, with live-in.

• Hard to escape any boyfriend sagas and other dramas in her private life.

• Lots of administration; you have to organise tax and NI payments, draw up a contract etc. and arrange insurance.

• Can sometimes work out the cheapest and easiest option for two children, fairly close in age.

• *Very* expensive for one child.

• Can often cope with children who would be too ill for minder or nursery.

• No formal back-up if nanny is too ill to work.

Nanny share (see also Chapter 5)

This is a useful compromise. It is a popular option for working women with one child, as arrangements become rather less easy with more. With many of the advantages of your own nanny, sharing with another family reduces cost dramatically. It can work with either a daily or live-in and can alternate between two houses to share the wear/bills. It can be a full-time share, or the week can be divided between families of part-timers. NB It is extremely important to ensure your needs and expectations dovetail. Sharers need full and frank discussion before going further!

How to find
- Word of mouth extremely important. Sharing relies heavily on local networking. Many successful shares come out of antenatal or postnatal exercise classes.
- Advertise locally, as you need someone living nearby.
- Many branches of the National Childbirth Trust run nanny share registers circulated to local members. Contact your nearest group.
- Your local Working Mothers Association group may run a register. Contact head office for details.
- Agencies: there are now several commercial agencies who specialise in putting compatible families in touch, and find the nanny. They advertise in *The Lady* and are usually listed in *Yellow Pages*.

Pros
- Much cheaper than employing your own nanny.

- Many nannies prefer (and stick with) this arrangement as they can earn more money and prefer to look after more than one child, once they are very experienced.
- Your child benefits from the company of a pal her age; only children get the nearest thing to a sibling.

Cons
- Your child won't get individual attention.
- You may have to invest in more expensive equipment, a double buggy for instance.
- Nanny is more restricted in her activities and especially expeditions, which are more difficult with two charges.

- The administrative element, particularly insurance, becomes more complex. Holiday planning can turn into a multi-dimensional nightmare.

Mother's helps (see also Chapter 5)

Not the same as a nanny. A mother's help is generally youngish, with no formal training in childcare and not much experience. Correspondingly she is cheaper and will do housework and help with the kids, but is not the best choice to be left in sole charge of younger children. The term nanny/mother's help can either mean a young, newly qualified nanny who is prepared to do some housework while she gains experience, OR an experienced but unqualified nanny who doesn't mind mucking in.

How to find
Same places as nannies, but you must make it clear exactly what you want. Advertising for a nanny/mother's help is too vague and rather over-optimistic if you really want an experienced NNEB to take sole charge of your tiny baby. Applicants can interpret this different ways and you may have to deal with a host of no-hopers. A qualified and experienced nanny would probably not be interested in doing any housework anyway.

Pros	Cons
• Much cheaper than a nanny and will do housework too.	• Untrained and probably inexperienced, so sole charge inadvisable for long periods. However, bear in mind that a sensible girl with young brothers and sisters has probably had more practical experience of childcare than a trained nanny fresh out of college.
• Ideal if you work from home and would be on hand to supervise.	
• Babysitting less of a problem.	• Young and possibly restless, likely to move on to improve experience and prospects.

Au pairs (see also Chapter 5)

Formally, an au pair is a single girl between 17 and 27, from Western Europe, who comes to live with your family to learn English. She can do light housework (up to five hours a day) for board, lodging and pocket money. The term 'au pair plus' refers to EC nationals who may take jobs in this country without a work permit and so can be employed normally as mother's helps.

How to find them

• Personal recommendation. Do you have friends in Europe who may know of daughters of their friends? Or even their daughter?
• Not guaranteed, of course, but if you learn of a super au pair working for a friend ask the au pair if there are any more at home like her!
• International organisations like the Round Table, or some churches have links abroad.
• St Patrick's International Youth Centre looks after the welfare of au pairs in Britain. Not an agency but may be able to help.
• Agencies: some nanny/domestic agencies have au pairs on their books, plus there are a number of specialists who can be found in *The Lady, Yellow Pages*. Also several agencies listed in *Working Holidays*, a guide to vacation jobs produced for students by the Central Bureau for Educational Visits and Exchanges.

Pros	Cons
• Wages negligible—pocket money only.	• Not an option for full-time care of babies or young children.
	• You have to provide food, heating, lighting etc., plus a possible extra large international phone bill!
• Will do some housework.	• Can only work five hours a day.
• Older children may find her helpful for language.	• You may find language a problem!
	• She may be more interested in learning English and having fun than looking after children.
• Lives in and can be expected to do regular babysitting.	• Corresponding loss of space and privacy. Unlike a nanny, an au pair should be treated like a member of the family as far as possible, eating with you and being introduced to your friends.
• With school age children au pairs come into their own.	• You bear considerable responsibility for her health and welfare and, to a lesser extent, education.
• A successful match can mean	

they become lifelong friends and
you can go and stay with them!

Nurseries (full time) (see also Chapter 6)

Most full-time nurseries are open 8–6, five days a week, practically
all year round. Fall into four categories: *Local authority nurseries*,
run by councils mainly for underprivileged and needy children, so
not an option for most working mothers, except possibly single
mums. *Workplace nurseries or creches*: provided by some large
employers, more frequently public sector organisations, and educational establishments. Employers subsidise the cost of places.
Private day nurseries: some are run by charities but most operate
as businesses, so vary enormously in quality. Staff can be nursery
nurses, teachers, playleaders or they may be unqualified. All nurseries must be registered with Social Services but do not assume
this, or that the high cost of some places is a guarantee of quality.
Most day nurseries take over-twos only and waiting lists exist at
many establishments. *Community nurseries*: can be used by anyone
in the local catchment area, not just priority cases. Partly funded,
they are run by a committee of parents and staff, so a certain
amount of time or commitment (e.g. for fund raising) is required.
Fees vary enormously (sometimes based on your income) but are
usually kept low.

How to find
● Start looking as early as possible, as places, rather than nur-
series, are often hard to find.
● All nurseries must be registered, so ask at your Social Services
Department for their official list.

Pros
● Usually open all year, apart
from Bank Holidays.
● Provide stimulating, lively
social atmosphere with some education too.
● Wide range of toys and activities (especially messy ones).
● Usually a healthy racial mix of
children.
● Don't have days 'off sick' or

Cons
● Opening times must be strictly
observed.
● Care isn't tailored to your
child's individual needs.

● Illness can spread rapidly and

suffer personal crises!

• Less risk of covert neglect or maltreatment as more adults about.

• Several different carers, so more relationships forged with a variety of adults.

• No administration, you just pay the bill.

regularly (meaning more time off for you, and you may catch it!).

• Less cosiness and exclusive cuddles.

• Some establishments charge a lot!

Part-time nursery care (see also Chapter 6)

Not usually suitable as sole form of care, but can be combined with nanny/childminder who takes and collects. Local Education Authority Nursery Schools are an introduction to school for children age three to five. Most have half-day sessions but some will offer a full day (until 3.30 pm). No charge.

Private schools offer half or full days for children two and a half upwards. Usually extremely expensive.

A fairly new concept is the extended day playgroup. Children over two and a half can be left with playgroup staff (who have been on playgroup courses) for up to eight hours a day, throughout the year. Mostly funded by local authority (therefore vulnerable) or charity. Parents pay small fee per session. Not yet widespread but may prove popular.

How to find
Contact Social Services Department or local reference library will have list of LEA and private nursery schools in the borough.

Pros
• A good way to help children prepare for school; provide education through play, lots of social contact and activity.

• A way of breaking up the day for older children at childminders or with nanny.

• No charge for LEA classes, low fees for playgroups.

Cons
• Places in LEA classes often hard to get—waiting lists exist.

• Private nursery schools very expensive—the most popular have children down on the waiting list from conception!

Care for School Age Children (see also Chapter 7)

Childminders

Some minders will take children on a part-time basis before and after school and it may be possible to extend this during the holidays. Social Services may help, or you could try advertising locally. 'After-school' children who are under eight will be included in the minder's 'official' quota, so places may be limited as part-timers cut down her earning power. Also, it's best to find a minder with an interest in older children.

'Piggyback nanny'

A version of a nanny share, but you only use someone else's full-time nanny for a few hours every day. OR if three families share a full-time nanny, those with school age children can pay for the hours they need. In this way holiday care is possible and the nanny gets a corresponding rise in pay. (See working example of a 'multi-share' in Chapter 5.)

Au pair

If you have room to spare, an au pair might solve your pre- and post-school problems. Cons are that many stay only for six months; also they cannot provide full-time holiday care, but they could be very useful ferrying children to and from other activities. However, young and timid girls may find controlling lively school kids a problem.

'Treasure'

An older version of the mother's help, possibly a local mum with grown-up children, whom you could employ to take children to and from school and give them tea. May be able to provide partial holiday care and might be willing to tackle some housework too.

Out-of-school schemes

Usually run from 3.30 to 6 pm during the week, some schemes also open throughout the holidays if they have suitable premises. Most 'kids' clubs' serve two or three local schools and provide a pick-up service, snack and drinks and various activities. Children are registered on arrival and are supervised throughout. Places are very hard to come by, waiting lists exist at many kids' clubs. Contact Social Service/Leisure and Amenities departments for local details, or try the Kids' Club Network (who keep a national list).

Holiday playschemes

Some schemes, which provide full-day supervised care, food and a variety of activities during the long summer holidays, are sponsored by large employers, others are run by voluntary groups, some are an extension of after-school clubs and some are organised each summer by local authorities. Contact your local Leisure and Amenities/Recreation department, or the Kids' Club Network.

Other holiday ideas include: employing a student or trainee (e.g. teacher, or NNEB hopeful) during their summer vacation (advertise at local colleges, references essential), sharing a nanny with a school teacher; residential holiday camps/adventure weekends for part of the time (can be pricey).

CHAPTER 4

The Truth About Childminders

Childminders are the most numerous, the worst paid and possibly the least understood of all British carers. We entrust more of our children to minders than to any other form of day care, while they are rewarded with a status somewhere between dinner lady and lavatory attendant (and a salary lower than either).

Minders themselves acknowledge the image problem, but point out it is only the occasional horror stories which reach the press, and which, sadly, linger in the public imagination. (A minder who saved the life of one of her charges through mouth-to-mouth resuscitation did not make the front pages.)

'Oh, I don't want a childminder,' stated a friend of mine, a first-time mother and otherwise highly intelligent, rational woman. 'They've all got Rottweilers under the stairs.' Several months and a nanny share fiasco later she still refuses to entertain the possibility of a minder, which means she is making the already difficult search for childcare harder still.

If *you* have previously dismissed having a childminder to care for your child for no better reason than you once heard or read something ghastly, perhaps you should examine your preconceived ideas.

The National Childminding Association (NCMA) was set up in 1977 to encourage professionalism in childminding and to win more respect for the minder. It is largely due to its efforts over the past decade that minding has been dragged from the dim recesses of smoky television rooms and presented realistically as a valid choice of day care. However, there is still a long way to go before childminding achieves the respect and funding it deserves.

There *are* bad minders, naturally, just as there are poor nannies and third-rate nurseries. Some minders are sloppy, lazy or basically uncommitted to their charges, but they are becoming rarer as more minders are encouraged to take up training opportunities and to adopt a more business-like approach. As standards rise, an undesirable carer is fairly easy to spot at first meeting, especially to the well-informed parent (see below).

The NCMA played an important role in advising the government for the relevant parts of the 1989 Children's Act. Local authorities now have to apply more stringent, and regular, checking and registration procedures. Many parents' worst fears about minders should be allayed by knowing that it is now illegal for a carer to smack a child. Also, the Act stresses the necessity for a carer to take into account the child's racial and cultural background—described by Jan Burnell, Director of the NCMA, as 'a real step forward in English law'.

This has now become part of the criteria to be applied when deciding who is a 'fit' person to be registered as a childminder. This usefully vague requirement can also be applied to measure aptitude, commitment and general suitability for childcare, and means that some form of pre-registration training will be mandatory.

However, it is you as a parent who have the most important part to play in the selection procedure. It must be stressed that leaving yourself plenty of time to find a suitable childminder is vital—you *must* see several before making a final choice. Don't listen to anyone official who says you must wait until shortly before returning to work. If anything, it's worth securing a place well in advance and paying a retainer until you need it.

Jenny Reid, a childminder with eight years experience, speaks on behalf of all minders who try to give a caring, professional service: 'Parents often spend more time choosing the family holiday than they do over their childcare provider. They opt for the first one they come across and then dismiss all care provided by registered childminders as poor, because of a bad experience which could have been avoided if they had taken more trouble in the first place.'

The advice in this chapter on how to conduct the initial interview and subsequent meetings has the full backing of the NCMA and will help you make the best-informed decision possible. It will also help you maintain a long and happy relationship with your minder.

THE 1989 CHILDREN ACT AND CHILDMINDING

Childminders and nurseries previously registered under the old system have to re-register with their local authority under the Act, which took effect from 14 October 1990. A childminder must now be registered for all children under eight whom she cares for in her own home for more than two hours per day for reward or payment.

She is allowed to care for (and her own children must be included):
- No more than three children under five (and some local authorities restrict the number of babies), or
- No more than six children aged five to seven years, or
- No more than six children under eight, of whom no more than three are under the age of five.

The local authority has the right to set a limit on the number of children over eight years.

The local authority has an annual duty to inspect all registered childminders, to check on the number of children, the maintenance and safety of premises and equipment *and* that the care provided reaches certain standards suggested in the Act. The local authority may add their own requirements to the nationally mandatory ones (for example, many authorities have now made it compulsory for childminders to take out public liability insurance and attend a pre-registration course). This means that basic requirements are the same everywhere, but standards will vary from region to region.

Why Choose a Childminder?

A good childminder—in other words a sensitive, caring professional—can provide a continuity of care unlike any other form of daycare. Unlike nannies, minders tend to be 'rooted' to an area, often through their husband's work and other family commitments. In some small communities, there are minders who attend the weddings of their grown-up charges, and then take on the second generation of babies! This may not be your desired aim, of course, but with some forward planning, it is possible for a successful minder to adapt to your child's changing needs, combining home-based care with part-time nursery classes and then taking and collecting your child from school.

Apart from the relative cheapness of this form of care, the flexibility of childminders is a major plus point too; many minders cater for shift workers, some will even take children overnight and at weekends. They will also do occasional overtime (if forewarned and adequately recompensed!).

A childminder can offer your child:

• Long-term, loving one-to-one care in a cosy home environment and familiar local neighbourhood, at a relatively low cost.

• Friendship of other children (her own, other minded children and those of friends and other local minders in her group).

• Education both in its broadest sense—gained from everyday activities around the home and out and about on local errands—and in a more structured way, with toys, paints, creative activities, all of which a good minder will provide.

• The opportunity for your child to learn about and to respect differences between people, families and cultures.

Naturally all minders have different ways of organising the day, depending on their commitments and the ages of the children in their care. But the two 'typical days' described below will give you some idea of what your child could be doing.

Marilyn Gilmartin from Bradford has been minding for over ten years. Her own daughters are 11 and 14. At present she has one full-time and one part-time child in her care. 'My day starts at 8 a.m., when the children arrive. The eldest are dropped off at school, then on Tuesdays I take the youngest to a local mother and toddler group where I help out. We're home around 12, have lunch and a sleep, and then you name it, out it comes, toys, games, the lot. Or sometimes we do household "tasks", like clearing out a cupboard (although it's always more untidy afterwards!).

'While this all sounds very ordinary and domestic, the difference between me and a full-time mum is that I can give my full attention to the child. If I think she is becoming bored with one thing, we can change activities—there's nothing I "have to finish first". I don't do any proper housework while the children are here (in fact I do very little at all!). You have to be prepared for your home to look like a wreck, it goes with the job! Some days we go into town and have lunch out as a treat. The children are learning all the time how to behave in public, to sit quietly and wait for me to fetch the food, all sorts of social manners. Other days we go for a walk to nearby fields, or visit the library.'

Barbara Almond from Doncaster has three teenage children of her own, and looks after a five year old and a 15-month-old girl, both of whom she has had since they were tiny babies, plus a boy, part time. Her working day starts at 7 am.

'The girls arrive and I give them breakfast, then my own children get up and get dressed. We go to school and drop off the eldest, then back at home all the toys come out. After that it's time for a nap before we go and pick up my part-time boy from nursery. We have lunch, then it's more toys, games, books, out to school and back again until everyone goes home at five. We have lots of occasional outings—coffee mornings, birthday parties, mother and toddler groups—with other members of the local childminding group and their children. We're a very social crowd.'

First Impressions

Learning about differences between people is important if your child is to develop as a sensitive and informed member of a multi-racial, multi-cultural, financially divided society. But what about you? You may be less prepared to come to terms with such differences than you think; especially when forced to confront them when first looking for a minder for your child.

Under the provisions of the 1989 Children Act childminders are recruited from all sections of society to reflect the diversity, not only in terms of ethnicity, religious and linguistic backgrounds, but also in terms of financial status and lifestyle. Some childminders you visit may not enjoy the same lifestyle as yourself; they may not live in such a 'posh' part of town. And even if they do, their homes may not look like yours.

If you are reading this as a brand new mum, your house has yet to suffer the ravages of children. Probably everything you have bought for the baby is squeaky clean, fluffy and perfect. The home of an experienced childminder, who throws herself wholeheartedly into the job, has had perhaps ten years of wear and tear from lively young children. Don't let this put you off—in fact it's a very good sign that children, not housework, come first.

When you visit childminders, try to clear your mind both of Mother-care adverts and press horror stories. Keep a tight rein on any ill-informed fears and notions about lifestyles and class. As long as you are satisfied with the basic hygiene and cleanliness, it's far more important to look for shared ideas about child development and discipline, good mothering skills and warm and friendly atmosphere.

However, in some inner-city areas, the differences in lifestyle may be too stark to reconcile, and childminding appears a less attractive option. Lucy Daniels, director of the Working Mothers Association, previously researched childminding in London and sums it up: 'You may live in a smart house in Southwark, but the chances are that most of the childminders will live in high rise blocks.'

If you can't bear the thought of your child in this situation, then clearly this arrangement is a non-starter. But the minder herself may have qualities which transcend all the practical disadvantages. Speaking from personal experience, I would not have believed anyone who told me that I would be happy leaving my one-year-old daughter in the care of someone who lived in a second-floor flat and kept an Alsatian.

I confess my heart sank when I first approached the flat and I nearly turned and ran when I heard loud barking. If I had, I would not have met the kind, caring woman who immediately put me and my daughter at ease. We chatted over a cup of tea and immediately 'clicked'; I watched my daughter rolling around happily with the other children and felt rather ashamed of myself. I even liked the dog, scrupulously trained and immensely gentle with all the children.

How to Find a Minder

Childminders, like parents and children, come in all shapes, sizes, ages and colours. One of the attractions of minding is its flexibility and uniquely private nature, and arrangements vary widely on hours and pay, although minimum guidelines exist. Officially, a childminder is a self-employed person who looks after children in her own home for more than two hours a day, for payment or reward. The law requires that she, or more rarely he, must be registered with the local Social Services department.

A childminder who is a member of the NCMA is far more likely to have undergone some childcare training, have insurance and be supported by a local group. NCMA members can also take advantage of the national association's telephone helpline, which is also open to parents. This can provide instant help and advice should any problem arise.

Where to start your search

Social Services should be your first port of call. The under-eights department of your local authority will have lists of all registered minders, and depending on how well organised/funded they are, will have up-to-date information on vacancies.

Often minders prefer to advertise in local newsagents or children's toy or clothes shops. Alternatively, place an advert yourself, giving brief details of hours needed and children's ages (it's not a good idea to give their names if you are giving a telephone number). You must ensure that any minders you see as a result of advertisements are registered and can show you up-to-date paperwork.

Some very successful minding arrangements begin informally, with a friend or neighbour offering their services. They must register before they begin, of course, which can take several months. Also, friendship complicates what is a business relationship and vice versa, so to avoid major fall-outs suggest your friend joins the NCMA and follows all their recommended business procedures, foremost among them having a contract.

Word-of-mouth recommendations—possibly the most reassuring way to find a minder, so wherever mothers gather, ask around. It's still advisable to follow the interview procedure and to see several minders before deciding—what suits one mum perfectly may leave you totally unimpressed!

Some enlightened employers now co-operate with local childcare services such as NCMA regional associations. In this way, they can provide information on vacancies or a 'matching service' for their employees. It's worth asking your boss or union representative if such a service exists in your company, and if not, why not? (See The Future on page 60.)

Meeting Your Minder

Once you have a list of three or four 'possibles', you can set up some meetings. These are not always easy situations for either parent or minder; the minder is on her home territory but is under intense scrutiny; parents are understandably anxious about making the right decision, while at the same time may be embarrassed about asking personal questions.

The following checklist of questions comes straight from the experts. It is reproduced from the NCMA's publication *A Parent's Guide to Childminding* which is available from them, price £1.50 (address on page 203). While everyone's requirements will vary, and you may have special concerns for your child, the NCMA list covers the important points. You may prefer to group them according to your priorities:

Hours minder works?
Flexible on picking-up times?
Cost per hour/week?
Overtime rates?
Cost for holidays and sickness?
Retainer needed?
Extra costs for food?
What training or experience does she have?
Is she insured?
Is she an NCMA member?
Does she attend a childminding group regularly?
Has pets?
Smokes?
Park nearby?
Playgroups nearby?
What other outings will she make?
What is her attitude to toilet training?
Other people who will be in the house?
Does she have a car?
Are car seats/safety belts fitted?
What does she feed the children?
Is she prepared to cater for special diets?
Does she have a back-up arrangement with another childminder in case she is ill?
Ages of her own children?
Ages of other children she looks after?
What is important to you about the way the children are cared for?
For example: does the childminder believe in using positive images of black and ethnic communities, does she allow war toys, are girls encouraged or discouraged from active, boisterous games, etc.
How many school children does she care for? (NB different local authorities will set different limits—you may discover there are rather too many for your liking who descend on the childminder after 4 pm!)

WHAT TO LOOK FOR IN THE CHILDMINDER'S HOME

- Do the other children seem happy and at ease?
- Is the house clean?
- Are pets under control?
- Are reasonable health and safety precautions being taken?
- Are there plenty of books and toys available?
- Are the children playing with them?
- Do the toys and books, and the minder herself, show a positive attitude to children of both sexes and of all races?
- Is there somewhere quiet for the children to rest?
- Is there a room reserved for the children's use?

Other specific points you may want to consider include reassuring yourself about accidents. Imagine a possible scenario—a fall from a park swing, a bang on the head—and ask the minder what she would do. Has she done any first-aid training?

It is also useful to know about equipment—will you be expected to provide a travel cot for daytime naps, for example? (The more stuff you have to lug to and fro the less attractive your choice will seem.) Does she have a double buggy (essential for outings with more than one baby/toddler)? If you decide to leave your child with her, how will this affect the organisation of outings, car trips etc? Has a new minder thought all this through?

You might like to add some questions about the rest of the childminder's family, too, as that can give you all sorts of clues about her attitude to child development. Politely asking what her husband does and (lightheartedly!) asking how he feels about her minding can be revealing too. If her family are not 100% behind her, a childminder is unlikely to stay the course. Also, while you may like the minder, you may not feel so sure about her partner. Seeing her own children helps you make a decision, too. Marilyn Gilmartin, who has the full support of her nearest and dearest, reassures parents by inviting them to meet all members of her family.

'I feel it's only fair, and perfectly reasonable for parents to know who, apart from me, is going to be coming into regular contact with their children when they are not around.'

Interview Techniques

Take care not to be too overbearing when interviewing a minder. Techniques of cross-examination are not appropriate; a friendly chat in which you both learn about each other is the level to maintain. It's just as important that the childminder warm to you, too, otherwise the relationship is a non-starter. Try to strike a balance. 'Parents who seem to know it all can be intimidating,' warns Sue Johnson, who has been minding for 15 years in north London and Enfield. 'A less experienced minder friend of mine admitted she felt "grilled" by one set of parents in what should have been a friendly interview, and rejected them because of this.'

Childminders should be prepared to show you around their home—or at least the rooms which the children will be using. You are entitled to ask about safety equipment such as fireguards and stairgates if such things are not in evidence. Even though the house will have been checked over by Social Services, don't relax your vigilance. Never accept less than the standards of safety you have in your own home.

'Be open and straightforward about the things you would like to see,' advises Jan Burnell, Director of the NCMA. 'Don't ask to use the loo and try to sneak a look around. Childminders do notice that kind of thing!'

Finding suitable childcare can be a nightmare; if you are running short of time it may become harder to consider finer points of etiquette after several fruitless interviews. But steamrolling ahead is not a good idea, nor is dropping in unannounced with the intention of catching a minder unawares. Firstly it's bad manners, and secondly, it won't really do you much good.

'You should always phone first,' says Sue Johnson. 'I've had people turn up on my doorstep without warning. I invited them in, but as it was a particularly lively time of day with all the children running around I couldn't give the parents my full attention. I prefer to arrange a first meeting during the day, perhaps while one or two of the children are asleep, so that parents can see the set-up. Then I suggest an evening meeting to sort out all the paperwork.'

Other ways to get off on the wrong foot include ringing up and immediately asking 'what do you charge?'. Obviously you need to know that you can afford the care, but as childminders' fees are universally low and tend to be similar throughout an area, it is better to ask the other vital question about the hours you need first. This might sound a touch precious, but consider it from a professional's point of view.

Lists of questions and issues to raise at interview are expected and approved by minders, who appreciate all efforts to treat them as professionals. What is less welcome are lists of what your child should and shouldn't do. Naturally you want to be sure that any special needs, dietary or otherwise, will be catered for, and the minder must know of any of your child's idiosyncrasies which might cause problems at first. But mums who expect the child-minder to behave like their personal nanny are in for a disappointment.

'I resent parents who think you are just there for their child,' admits Sue. 'They issue precise instructions about when to feed and sleep and don't seem to realise that the child must fit into your routine, which has been carefully devised to suit all the children.'

Don't ignore your instincts. Often your wisest choice is the minder whose home didn't quite match up to your ideal, but whose company you really enjoyed. You can't say why, but you just know your child will be happy there. Jan Burnell: 'Mums often use the term "gut feeling" when they sense, rather than can explain, why a particular childminder will be right for their child. But what they are doing is picking up on tiny clues from behaviour, body language, tones of voice, general atmosphere. These are perfectly valid pieces of evidence, so trust your innermost feelings. You will know what's right when you find it.'

Jan Burnell advises visiting at least three minders before reaching a decision. Ideally you should go back and see your chosen minder again to reassure yourself that you are right, and to complete all the formalities.

'There should always be a contract, with both parties keeping a copy and absolutely clear on the details,' recommends Jan. 'Parents should check that the minder is an NCMA member—around half of all registered minders are—and if she has public liability insurance. This is vital, and parents should insist on it. It's not there just for the rare and tragic accidents, but for smaller items like a lost coat, or a stolen buggy. NCMA members can take advantage of a very good scheme we arranged for them at a very low annual premium. Knowing who will pay up in small but aggravating incidents takes a lot of tension and hostility out of the relationship.'

The Working Relationship

In the best interests of your child, the parent/minder relationship should develop as a partnership, with both of you sharing in your child's development. This is why establishing common ground and attitudes to discipline, education etc. are so important at the interview stage. A strong and healthy partnership demands respect on both sides; you must acknowledge the minder's experience and training, but that doesn't mean you have to accept something which makes you unhappy. You must make your feelings clear to the childminder, however tricky you find it.

Jan Burnell acknowledges that leaving your child in someone else's home complicates the issue. Parents find it difficult to be as assertive about their child's needs as they would be if the child were in a more impersonal group setting.

'It can be difficult enough making a complaint to a nursery teacher; it's even harder with a childminder because she is often seen, quite wrongly, as a substitute mother. Viewing the relationship this way is asking for trouble. It can lead parents to feel they are attacking the minder's own mothering skills if they criticise something and the childminder may also take it this way. If both sides regard childminding as a professional service within which complaints can be aired and improvements made, this avoids a lot of heartache later on.'

Jenny Reid from Cumbria has had several long and stable minding arrangements. She admits she becomes very attached to most of her minded children, but not as a mother figure: 'There is an element of bonding, somewhere between being an auntie or a grannie.' Minder Barbara Almond feels differently: 'I would describe myself more as a good friend to the kids, a person they can trust and rely on. I think you should encourage professional distance, but you do get very involved with some families. I've just become Godmother to one of the little girls.'

'Maintaining a good relationship with parents is one of the things we stress on all our training courses,' says Jan Burnell. 'Childminders must be willing to take on board how parents may be feeling about separation from their children, and their natural anxieties about the standard of care on offer. Part of our training asks minders to examine honestly how they feel about working mothers; a minder who secretly disapproves should not be looking after other people's children.'

Jenny Reid has learned over her eight years of minding to make allowances for the occasional rough patches with some parents. 'I think you have to acknowledge the feeling of inadequacy that some working mothers suffer from when it comes to their children. They often compensate by being overcritical and unwilling to trust you at first. It's more than guilt, it's a form of grief at being separated. You must sympathise with mothers, not criticise.'

What Really Makes a Minder Mad!

A minder's tolerance will only stretch so far and, sadly, far too many parents abuse the relationship. Because childminders become very attached to children in their care and go out of their way to protect them, they are vulnerable to exploitation. Top of the list of minders' grumbles are parents who are constantly late picking up their children.

'Sometimes the demands of parents' work conflict with the need to collect the children, and I'm afraid the children don't always come first,' says Barbara Almond. 'I can sympathise when a working mum, already on dodgy ground with her boss, doesn't want to make a fuss over some unexpected overtime. But surely she could take just two minutes to phone me and let me know? In the past, I've had some mothers turn up over an hour late saying "I couldn't get near a phone". The bottom line is they know I can't leave their child with anyone else, even if it means missing appointments of mine or my family's.'

Listening to minders recall their worst experiences is a shaming experience for a working mother. It's hard to believe that some women could so blatantly take advantage of the childminder's attachment to their children. 'I've had several "difficult payers" over the years,' recalls Jenny Reid. 'The worst experience with one family was when over a period of three months payment for childminding came a poor second to the purchase of luxury household goods. The first time I was dumb-struck when they told me they had just bought a video, so "could they pay next week?". To my amazement they did it again next pay day. However—third time lucky—I was ready and, complete with bill in hand, got there first. The family never did it again. I could have cancelled our contract on the strength of non-payment, but as is usually the case, it's the child who suffers in the end, either from chopping and changing minders or by the bad feeling between family and minder. But I would never let it happen to me again.'

Marilyn Gilmartin can now laugh when she remembers an early incident when a rather unreliable mother just didn't turn up at all one evening. 'It was awful at the time, these poor kids sitting there until 8 pm and I had no idea what had happened—there was no reply from her home. She eventually rolled up, smelling strongly of drink after celebrating her birthday with girls from the office. She claimed her husband was supposed to have picked up the kids, but he forgot!'

Parents who quibble about paying the full amount for their holidays, Bank Holidays and occasional sickness can do irreparable damage to the relationship. Disputes over holiday pay are common, says Jan Burnell, as many parents believe that as the minder is self employed, she has to take the rough with the smooth.

'I advise minders to point out that other self-employed workers charge their weekly fee just as a call out!' says Jan. 'Comparing their charges to a plumber's puts things in perspective.'

How to Make Your Minder's Day!

Apart from the basic courtesies of paying on time and picking up promptly (and soberly) on time, how can a working mother keep her childminder happy?

'What really helps is a thank you at the end of the day, which makes you feel appreciated,' says Barbara Almond. 'Plus a bit of consideration by warning of lateness—I am willing to be flexible if I have enough notice, and extra payment, of course, if this is to be a regular occurrence.'

Barbara says that she doesn't expect presents, while Sue Johnson admits that a bunch of flowers out of the blue really cheers her up. 'Many parents don't bother to ask "how was your day", although they're only too willing to tell you about their row with the boss.' If you don't show any interest in the childminder's day, it can lead to some bitterness. 'Some minders will feel they are taken for granted,' warns Sue. 'They start thinking "you'd appreciate my job if you'd ever done it yourself."'

It's a good idea to stipulate in the childminding contract that both mother and minder get together regularly to discuss any problems which may arise. It's not worth letting small niggles grow to destructive proportions, as this could eventually affect your child. Sue Priest of the Birmingham Childminding Association admits frankly: 'However professional you are, if you have negative feelings about the parents it can affect your attitude to the children, even unconsciously.'

On a more subtle level, if your minder seems a bit offhand sometimes, with no obvious cause, try seeing yourself through her eyes. This proved a salutary experience for one working mother who was having her cake and eating it: 'After a good day at work, I am filled with energy and confidence and arrive at the childminders quite full of myself and longing to whisk my daughter away for our magic hour before bedtime. One occasion I arrived feeling life was wonderful . . . and I couldn't understand why my childminder wasn't filled with the same enthusiasm or keen to hear about my triumphs. Then I saw it from her point of view. Now I make a point of playing down my day and instead ask about hers, showing an interest in her family and complimenting her whenever possible. I think our relationship has improved now I am a little more sensitive and she feels appreciated.'

Many of the working mothers who answered the questionnaire prepared for this book had established successful relationships with their minders. This is a selection of what they have learned from their experiences:

Britta from Coventry: 'I consider my minder Terri to be a friend. She has looked after my son Vladimir, now five, since he was one year old. We have shared Vladi's upbringing, and I make sure that she is involved in decisions affecting her. I never want to impose.'

Kim from Sussex works for the Civil Service and leaves both her children with the wife of her husband's colleague who is a registered minder. 'You need understanding and respect on both sides, a clear understanding of important issues. I always say thank you, even though I pay her. I repeat all the nice things the kids say about her.'

Jacqueline Gantley, a part-time partner in a general practice, shares the care of Catrin, four, and Daniel, two, between a minder and grandparents. She advises: 'Treat your carer as an individual with needs, too.'

Jane, a lecturer at a Further Education college in southwest

London, had to go on a waiting list for her popular minder! Now she has excellent care she wants to keep it. 'I try to let her know what an essential role she plays. I never take liberties or take her for granted. She is always invited to the children's birthday parties, and I do give her the occasional bunch of flowers.'

Julie Lock, a secretary/PA from Bristol, has used a childminder for the past three years for Kelly, seven, and Ashley, five. The minder was, and still is (!) a friend. 'The most important aspect of the relationship is honesty. If either of us has a problem we sit down over a coffee and discuss it. I always feel relieved, even if we don't actually solve the problem.'

Susan Robertson from Chester, an FE lecturer, has used a childminder for her son Andrew, five, for the past four and a half years very happily: 'Never take your carer for granted. Always tell them well in advance when you're going to be late. Don't expect them to drop everything for you, they have busy lives too. Make sure you have a similar outlook before you start. We spent a whole evening with her family before Andrew was born!'

Elizabeth Higgins, a health contracts manager from East London, used a minder full time for two years before embarking on a job share. She recommends: 'a determination not to quibble about money, flexibility on both sides over hours and holidays. A relationship as friends and equals.'

Christine, a civil servant from Middlesex, has used the same minder for 11 years: 'It is more a way of life for her than a means of earning a living. She has become a friend, and the children probably feel part of her family.'

Sally Jane Maloney, a director of a computer systems company, was so happy with her minder that she brought forward plans to have a second child because her minder had a place coming up! 'You must realise that the childminder is a professional too and should be treated with respect. Listen to her advice, however adamant you are that your way is best. Be flexible—don't place too many constraints on her by forbidding *all* sweets, cakes, etc. My minder has to cater for Muslims and vegetarians and it's not easy to plan menus if parents are too heavy on the rules.'

Marilyn, a part-time picture researcher from Harlow, Essex, found a minder with 20 years experience for her daughter Amy Louise: 'She not only cares for the children physically, but is also very interested in their mental development. She believes in providing plenty of stimulating activities—visits, reading, etc. She devotes

all her time to the children and they respond very well to this
involvement.'

Finally, *Rachel Pike* who successfully nominated her childminder
Monica Hayden as a winner of the *SHE* Working Mothers' Thank
You Award sums up the qualities to look for in your minder: 'The
ideal qualities of a childminder must be to give the parents peace
of mind while away from their children; to know that they are
receiving the best possible attention in a safe, caring environment
with just the right amount of discipline. Monica's door is always
"open" even at 2 am when baby Mark decided to arrive! Simon,
four, and Mark, ten months, have been with her since they were
four months old. She exudes love and warmth and means so much
to us that she's also Mark's Godmother. "Aunty Mon" is one in
a million.'

The Future—A More Business-Like Approach

In the forefront of change is Childminding In Business! Ltd (CIB!
Ltd), the consultancy service of the National Childminding Association. CIB! Ltd has been responsible for the development and
implementation of most of the major childminding networks in the
country, such as those now used by several health and education
services. The success of the network set up by CIB! Ltd for Allied
Dunbar plc in Swindon may well persuade more private sector
employers.

The mainspring of a childminding network is a professional co-
ordinator, trained and supervised by CIB! Ltd. On the employer's
behalf, the co-ordinator brings childminders and employees and
their children together. She or he finds and assesses registered childminders who meet the criteria laid out in the CIB! Ltd 'Quality
Charter'. Co-ordinators also visit childminders once a month to
monitor quality of care, safety and health procedures according to
an exacting set of rules. Initial and on-going training is provided
for the minders, as well as a toy library and equipment loan scheme
to enhance standards of care. An emergency back-up service can
take over if a minder is ill or on holiday.

This way of offering childcare for employees is relatively inexpensive for a company to set up. It makes choosing a childminder
a more attractive option for many working mothers; the initial
hassle of finding and interviewing prospective minders is eased

tremendously with the help of a co-ordinator who will pre-select three or four appropriate choices after listening to parents' needs. Peace of mind can be gained from the assessment and monitoring service.

Partnerships between employers and Social Services departments to create similar schemes can also be a valuable option. Elida Gibbs in Leeds have seconded an Under-Eights Advisor to implement their childminding network, which functions in the same way as the CIB! Ltd networks.

At present, no childminding subsidies are paid by employers to parents using these networks, but an increasing number of employers now offer Childcare Vouchers (which are endorsed by the NCMA) for employees to use with registered childminders.

The NCMA is now working with Childcare Solutions, a new service for employers and working parents, launched in February 1992. It is a nationwide database of childcare facilities for member employers, who pay an annual subscription. This can provide general details of childcare in a given area, for the benefit of firms who are either relocating or transferring staff members.

In addition, nominated employees will be able to phone a special number with their individual childcare requirements, and Childcare Solutions will 'match' them with a carer on the files. If a childminder is requested, the NCMA will suggest suitable minders with vacancies, using information gained from their regional groups. The service is also linked to several nanny agencies, and has a huge national list of private day nurseries.

If your employer's attitude to providing childcare has previously been lukewarm, these new ideas may be greeted with more enthusiasm. A childminding network can be established at a fraction of the cost of a workplace nursery, for example, and requires minimal involvement on the part of the employer. Why not have a word with the personnel department and point them in the right direction?

CHAPTER 5

When You Are the Boss: Nannies, Mothers' Helps and Au Pairs

Employing someone to care for your child in your own home means (in theory!) you can call the shots. You have greater control, more authority and a far more flexible arrangement than a child-minder or nursery can offer. You are also landed with one of the most nerve-wracking choices of your life. Agencies may vet, past employers can recommend, but when it comes to hiring a nanny the ultimate responsibility is yours. Not without reason does Isobel McKenzie Price, an experienced boss and mother of three, describe choosing a nanny as 'the worst decision I've ever had to make!'

Take heart, after a couple of false starts Isobel now has a 'wonderful' nanny, who has looked after her two daughters for over three years, and is about to take the third baby under her wing. Isobel, a magazine editor, and her nanny Antoinette have both learnt a lot from past experiences as employer and employee, which have contributed to their current, enviably solid working relationship. They, and other working mothers and nannies, offer some valuable observations in this chapter.

It is often said that nannies don't provide good continuity of care because they are always moving on; part of this is to do with the lack of a career structure, but a lot of nannies flit because their basic needs and feelings are ignored by insensitive (or inexperienced) employers, or they are just plain exploited. Don't make that mistake: a caring and professional nanny can be your greatest ally, she will enable you to work with complete peace of mind and make your children's lives happy and secure. A combination of luck and good recruitment practice (including scrupulous vetting) will help you find her in the first place, and most importantly, guard you against the 'Nanny from Hell'.

During the compilation of this book, several horrifying cases came to light of nannies injuring and even, in America, murdering children in their care. In Britain, 'nanny' Carol Withers was finally sent to prison after fracturing the skulls of two babies in her care;

masquerading as an NNEB-trained maternity nurse she had lied about her qualifications and managed to con not one employer but two. Both families, sadder but wiser, realise now that they should have thoroughly checked before accepting this confident, well-presented woman at face value.

At present, without any form of legislation or registration procedure for nannies, the onus is on you as an employer to choose wisely. Much of this comes down to your basic intuition, but you must also follow up references assiduously. If you are contemplating employing a nanny for the first time this can seem a daunting task. However, there are tried and trusted ways to thoroughly vet a prospective nanny, and these are detailed below. Mad and bad nannies are few and far between, but you must be aware that they are out there.

Learning by other mothers' mistakes, not all as calamitous as those mentioned above, will help you avoid a good many yourself. Often it's not finding a good nanny but keeping one which is the problem. While there is no substitute for experience, it really helps to talk to as many people as possible before entering the fray.

The advice from mothers, nannies and agencies in this chapter is geared towards the first-timer (although if you're on your fifth nanny in as many months it may help you discover where you're going wrong!). It covers the dos and don'ts of advertising, using agencies, interviewing and following up references, and provides vital clues to the secret of maintaining a sensitive, professional and long-term working relationship.

Who Does What?

To the uninitiated, various terms like nanny/mother's help and au pair plus can be baffling. There *are* important distinctions, particularly over such sensitive areas as housework, and significant differences in pay. A highly qualified and experienced nanny will not lift a duster to help you outside the children's bedroom and will be amazed that you dared suggest it. To save you time and money (and to spare you the withering scorn of a nanny agency supremo), here are the generally accepted definitions:

Nanny: a qualified (usually NNEB, see page 67) carer. The fully fledged variety will have had several years experience and will expect to be paid accordingly. A 'proper' nanny's duties cover all routine daily care and entertainment of the children, including outings, collecting older children from school/playgroup, ferrying between various other social activities. Nannies expect to keep the children's room (and their own, if they live in) clean, and to be responsible *only* for the children's washing, shopping and cooking. **Nanny share**: in order to afford the sort of qualified and experienced nanny described above, many working mothers decide to split both a full-time carer and the cost. This is usually between two families, but can be more, in which case the nanny is obliged to register with the local authority. Permutations are many and various (see below under Sharing a Nanny); this is becoming an increasingly popular option for working mothers and experienced nannies, who often prefer these jobs because of the extra challenge and money.

Nanny/mother's help: often a live-in position, this can either be a) a newly qualified nanny with no experience, usually very young, who is prepared to take on *some* housework in order to gain experience and her first reference, or b) an unqualified, but experienced woman who has looked after children (possibly lots of younger brothers and sisters) and has less dignity to stand on. Many mothers say that they have found experience more valuable than formal training, but if you are leaving a tiny baby for the first time it's probably wiser to choose someone with both.

Mother's help: someone with no formal qualifications who expects to work *with* a mother, helping out with both housework and children. A good choice if you work from home and want someone to keep children happy and occupied within earshot. Mother's help could also apply to a mature woman living locally, who could collect your school age children and tackle some housework too. Under the 'Working Holidaymaker' scheme, an Australian, New Zealander or Canadian aged 17–27 can work for up to two years in this country. Australians and New Zealanders, particularly those with some childcare experience, are a popular choice with many mothers who find their cheerful and easy-going attitude extremely helpful!

Au pair: officially a single woman with no dependents, aged between 17–27, who comes to this country to learn English and to live with an English-speaking family. She is allowed to do up to five hours 'light housework' and childcare for pocket money. If she is not an EC national, the longest an au pair can stay is two years, but she will have to register with the police after six months, and have her passport restamped. For the part-time care of school children an au pair can help ease your burden, otherwise not really an option, certainly not for sole charge of babies or toddlers. The easiest way to find an au pair is through an agency which specialises in them, which means they have a network of European contacts who recruit girls abroad. Alternatively you can advertise or contact other organisations direct (see addresses on page 204).

Au pair plus: this term usually describes a girl from the EC who can come to work in Britain free of the restrictions described above, or a British girl filling in time before going to college. While in essence a fair enough idea, it often leads to exploitation. Using these young women as a form of cheap household labour is frowned upon by most reputable agencies, who say the combination of inexperience and overwork usually ends in disaster, particularly when children are involved.

Experience Versus Qualifications

Mothers who have employed nannies from both categories swear by experience. Smaller local agencies, who are in touch with grass root feeling, also back this up. 'Mothers don't want a starchy matron,' comments Dornier Whittaker, who handles the nanny side of London domestic agency South of the River. After over 18 years in business the agency has seen a rise in demand for nanny/mother's helps, experienced with children but also prepared to join in the daily maintenance of a lively, informal household. 'Most mums want somebody younger than themselves, so they don't feel intimidated, particularly if they're not used to handling staff', says Dornier. 'We now find there's a lot of demand for New Zealand and Australian girls, who are far less finicky than English nannies about what they will or will not do.'

General experience of life, which gives independence and common sense, is far more important than an intimate knowledge of potty training when it comes to getting along with an employer. That precious but elusive quality, maturity, *may* be present in an exceptional 18-year-old NNEB graduate who has left home (where she looked after younger siblings), has seen something of the outside world and understands that washing up doesn't disappear by magic, but don't count on it. ('The NNEB course doesn't teach things like clearing away your own orange peel, always taking your empty coffee cup to the sink and not putting your feet up on the furniture,' sighed one employer-ravaged agency boss.)

After employing two NNEB-trained, but very young and tender nannies, Isobel McKenzie Price is now convinced that it's experience and maturity which really count. 'Both my first nannies were straight from college; they were dailies, but they lived at home with mum. They knew all their childcare theory but they had no experience of running a home—they still had everything done for them. They regarded nannying as a nine-to-five job, and they were both very into the nanny circuit—socialising was top priority which ultimately ended in disaster.'

A liking for company is understandable, particularly in 18 year olds, and a sensible mother will make sure her nanny joins a local circle to prevent loneliness and boredom. In Isobel's case, her second nanny joined a group of nannies looking after children of various ages who all played together. Harmless enough, except that Isobel's young nanny lacked the experience to realise that her 18-month-old charge Arcadia should be supervised with the older, rougher children.

'I came home from work to discover the nanny in a terrible panic. Apparently while she and her pals had been gossiping over coffee, one of the children had picked up Arcadia like a doll and dropped her—now she couldn't walk and seemed to be in great pain.'

Fortunately X-rays showed no physical damage. But Arcadia was so terrified by the episode it took her several months to learn to walk again. 'That nanny was about to leave, which saved me from sacking her,' says Isobel, who can now be philosophical about the incident, although she hasn't forgotten the anxious hours in Casualty. 'It was an accident, I know. She was distraught and she learnt a lesson. It could have been worse; she was young and silly, but at least she was sane. One of my friends came home from a hard day at the office to be told by her new NNEB that her ten-month-old son "was possessed by the devil"!'

To fill the gap, Isobel employed her cousin Annie, who had nursing training. The two women became immensely close, and Annie was present at the birth of Isobel's second daughter Ella. Having someone looking after the children whom she and they really like, with maturity and a sense of humour, helped Isobel realise what she had been missing!

Her current nanny Antoinette has been with the family for over three years. She is 24, with no formal qualifications but several years experience gained from working with two large Irish families, where she was expected to cope with all the housework and several lively children. Having really earned her spurs the hard way, Antoinette had loads of commonsense and practical experience and had her own life sorted out by the time she came to work in London.

Antoinette also had the other personal qualities for which Isobel was searching: 'I wanted someone who could go that extra mile, somebody with a bit of nous. A nanny has to step into your shoes when you're not there, react as you would in all sorts of situations, most critically if there is an accident. It's a job which demands maturity, independence of thought and action. I liked Antoinette immediately at the interview and felt I could trust her to look after my children. But most of all I was reassured by the fact that she could so obviously look after herself.'

The NNEB—What Does it Mean?

There are plenty of working mothers, particularly of first babies, who want a trained as well as experienced nanny. The most commonly held nannying qualification is the National Nursery Examination Board's Diploma (formerly certificate) in nursery nursing which is known in convenient if illogical shorthand as 'the NNEB', while a diploma holder is 'an NNEB'.

The full-time course is offered at colleges of further education around the country and five fee paying colleges, including the 'Big Three'—Norland, Chiltern and Princess Christian—who add extra qualifications after further study, including the Royal Society of Health Diploma of Nursery Nursing. NNEB students at the non-residential London Montessori Centre also study for the Montessori Childcare and Teaching Diploma simultaneously.

If you are preparing to pay for a qualified nanny, you might find it reassuring to know what you're paying for. The NNEB syllabus is presently being restructured into more flexible, competence-based modules, but in addition to detailed observation of children and practical experience (supervised placements in a variety of settings: nurseries, hospitals, private homes etc.) the two-year course will continue to cover the following areas:

- Children's growth and stages of development.

- Physical development, including health, safety, clothing, footwear, baby equipment, nutrition, childhood illnesses, first aid, care of sick children, children with special needs.
- Cognitive development and how to assist that development through stimulation and learning through play.
- Emotional development.
- Social relationships, which includes a wider look at the family in society.
- The rights and responsibilities of children and the family, which gives students a basic understanding of family law, and the workings of Social Services, health and education.
- The Meaning of Professionalism, which covers employment both as a nursery nurse in the public and private sector and as a private nanny. Topics covered include coping with the 'particular stress' of being a nanny—for example loneliness, long hours and the adaptability needed to live with a family, in addition to spelling out the responsibilities of an employer vis-à-vis tax and national insurance.

The whole care training sector is undergoing dramatic fluctuation as the National Council for Vocational Qualifications introduces changes to the structure of many courses, including the NNEB. If you wish to know more about an unfamiliar qualification, contact the college which awarded it.

Live In or Out?

There are pros and cons attached to each. A daily nanny will cost you more in salary terms, but she is likely to be more mature and experienced, particularly if she has moved out of her family home and is running her own life. Her hours will be shorter and she is unlikely to accept much extra babysitting without prior warning and extra payment. You keep your privacy at evenings and weekends and she has her independence.

However, if you have a job where late/early work is unavoidable and regular, you may decide that a live-in nanny can provide the most flexible cover, especially while your children are tiny. A live-in will also be available for some babysitting and possibly the occasional night duty if you agree this in advance and pay a generous bonus. You need to have sufficient space in your house to offer her privacy and peace and quiet, but the accommodation doesn't have to be terribly grand.

Jane, who worked at the time in a merchant bank, sometimes until 10 pm, speaks very highly of her live-in nanny Helen whom she employed to look after her son William, then one and a half. Although Jane and her husband didn't live in a huge house (in fact a three-bedroomed London terrace) the live-in relationship worked because all parties were sensitive to each other's needs.

'Helen always knew when to disappear!' Jane remembers. 'At 21 she was mature enough to slip away if a row was brewing between my husband John and myself. We made it clear that she was expected to spend most evenings in her room, and I'm sure she preferred that, but if John worked late I'd usually ask her if she wanted to watch a film with me downstairs. We tried not to exclude her—for example if John was getting a takeaway on Friday night we'd call up and see if she wanted to join us. On Sundays she would help cook and eat lunch with the family.

'I told her right from the start that she was an essential part of the household, that I *needed* her in order to do my job, that she wasn't a luxury. Her last job was as live-in assistant to what I call an "idle rich" mother, and although she'd lived in a beautiful house in Chelsea and gone on exotic holidays, Helen told me she felt I appreciated her professional skills. "This is for real" is how she put it.'

But however well handled, you do sacrifice privacy with a live-in. Jane admits that her husband felt the strain more than she did. As a lecturer in an FE college, he had longer than average holidays and sometimes missed the freedom of being totally alone in the house. 'I think it's harder for a man,' says Jane. 'He has to always check the coast is clear before dashing out of the bathroom in his boxer shorts, and he may not feel relaxed having breakfast in his dressing gown. Imagine how we'd feel with another man around the house all the time!'

How to Find a Nanny

Before you actually start to look for a nanny decide exactly what the job will entail. Journalist Alexandra Campbell, mother of twins Rosie and Freddy, knew that the family's extra requirements would have to be spelt out to a prospective carer. 'I sat down and wrote

a detailed list—four pages in all—of exactly what I wanted a nanny
to do, and clarifying how the nanny would be compensated when
I was late home from work, her holidays, pay, all sorts of "what
ifs". In addition to nursery duties, I specified three extra household
things which I decided I couldn't bear any fuss over—to empty the
dishwasher and the washing machine and to nip down to the corner
shop when required. This list formed the basis of the interview, and
then finally the contract, which also clearly spelt out the instantly
sackable offences, such as drug taking, drinking, having men in the
house while on duty, theft (including shoplifting), exposing the
babies to danger. Having that down in black and white meant my
nanny read, understood and signed her agreement, without me
having to raise these rather embarrassing but necessary points.'

Her nanny Lisa has since admitted that she took the job partly
because Alexandra had been so clear and straightforward about
everything, unlike her previous employers. Alexandra has nothing
but praise for her, and Lisa is very obviously a 'catch'; when Alexandra put her house on the market a young couple who looked
round said they were prepared to make an offer 'if nanny is
included'!

When to start looking

As a rough guide, it will take about six weeks to advertise, interview and wait for a nanny to complete her notice. This varies, of
course, some nannies can start immediately, while if you advertise
at a traditionally lean time of year, i.e. just before Christmas, you
may have to repeat the whole procedure. If you're feeling nervous,
it might be reassuring to book two weeks at once.

Remember that if you are advertising in the press you are bound
by deadlines: eight days (or 15 if you miss press day) in *The Lady*,
for example, possibly weekly for a local newspaper. You may well
be advertising in a panic, but if the worst comes to the worst, it's
better to use a nanny from a temporary agency, even if it is expensive, than rush your selection procedure and make an even more
costly mistake.

Where to advertise

If you live in a nanny-dense suburb, try a card in a local newsagent's
window, or popular toy or children's clothes shop. This is a good

way of finding a local girl who will live out, possibly more mature and experienced. It's a sensible place to advertise a nanny share, as these work best when families live in close proximity.

The local paper may also attract a conveniently local girl. It's also good for nanny shares and possibly to attract a more mature 'mother's help' type of woman to pop in daily. If you want to advertise nationally *the* place is *The Lady* magazine, read by a great many nannies. It is published Thursdays, available on Wednesday. Not so good if you're in a tearing hurry to find someone, but it casts your net far more widely, particularly if you're looking for a live-in. Written advertisements only are accepted. *Nursery World*, published fortnightly, is aimed more at nursery nurses, but does carry some advertisements for private nannies. Both magazines carry Situations Wanted, too. See page 204 for the addresses.

WARNING NOTE

In all advertising concerning children, it's best not to give their names if you are including a telephone number, as crank callers have been traced to adverts in *The Lady*, for example. Box numbers give more privacy, but attract fewer applicants and take longer. Beware of giving away too much information in the newsagent's window, as well.

Other ideas

If you are willing to take on a newly qualified nanny, you could try contacting a college near you which offers the NNEB course. (A list of colleges is available from the NNEB head office—see page 204 for the address). For those with grandiose schemes, you may like to know that Norland College has its own employment agency which takes up a reference on *you*. Demand far exceeds supply. Chiltern and Princess Christian will enter your details on file and pass them on to any of their nannies looking for work. Contact all the colleges direct.

What to say in your advertisement

The general view seems to be don't bother making it all sound wonderful—be absolutely straightforward and add a bit of colour with a well-chosen adjective (about the job, not your 'adorable' or 'fun-loving' children!) if you want to make it look a bit more friendly. Nannies say they are attracted by the tone of an advertisement, so communicate a little flavour of your family life which might connect with nannies on a similar wavelength. Essentials to include are:

- The type of help you need (be specific, see Who Does What? on page 63), whether live in or out, whether qualified/experienced.
- Number, age and sex of children.
- Duties, for example only nursery, or some housework included.
- Specific requirements/exclusions, e.g. non-smoker, minimum age or experience, driver or own car required.
- What you have to offer—in terms of accommodation (own room/shower, TV, etc.) and attractive perks: time off, use of car/ swimming pool, chance to travel.
- Starting date.

Opinions differ on whether or not to include a salary. Experienced nanny-sharers who can put up quite a tidy sum between them say they will name the amount, other mums prefer to leave their options open until the interview stage. All agree, however, that writing 'attractive salary' is a waste of time and money. 'Cleaner employed' will reassure a nanny on the domestic dilemma.

Below are two very different examples from *The Lady*:

LIVE IN NANNY, WINCHESTER: Cheerful and responsible sole charge nanny needed for girl (4) at school and boy (1) in friendly home. NNEB preferred/experienced with toddlers. Weekends and most evenings free. Own sunny room/TV. Non-smoker and driver essential. Long term. Box No 0000

DAILY NANNY for boy (2½) girl (7 months). Non-smoker. NNEB/ exp. Refs essential. Queens Park. Tel. 000000

Using an Agency: Choose With Care!

Many mothers dislike the randomness of advertising and approach an agency, thus hoping to cut down most of the selection procedure. It must be stressed, however, that **you must vet an agency as thoroughly as a prospective nanny, and you must still follow up references of your chosen candidate personally.**

If you don't hear of any through personal recommendation,

agencies can be found through your *Yellow Pages* (local ones will be useful for supplying live-out nannies within easy distance); or look through advertisements in *The Lady* and *Nursery World*. The Federation of Recruitment and Employment Services (see below) will send out a list of approved agencies on request. However, while there are many excellent recruitment agencies throughout the country, who offer a professional and conscientious service, there *are* those whose amateur and irresponsible practices are actually putting children and families at risk.

Susan Wasmuth, proprietor of the long-established Pre-Select Nanny Agency in Birmingham, is in the forefront of those within the business calling for tighter rules to govern the issuing of licences to recruitment agencies, particularly those agencies who specialise in supplying staff to work with children. These would include making it compulsory for agencies to *personally* interview and vet all applicants, and to be able to consult the police computers to check for any history of child abuse, fraud or theft.

As a qualified employment consultant and working mother herself, Sue is particularly worried by an upsurge of new, less professional agencies who are often more concerned to cash in on the increasing demand from working mothers rather than providing a reliable service. She is also scathing about au pair agencies, describing the market as 'a total lottery'. Her advice to parents is to ask a lot of tough questions before signing on with any agency, and preferably use one that has been personally recommended.

'Far too many agencies are run by people with no previous experience or qualifications. They don't bother to interview applicants personally or check up on references, even when sending out staff to work with tiny babies. When first approaching an agency you should ask if any of the staff hold a certificate of recruitment practice, if they interview all applicants personally and ask how they follow up references.'

A good agency also acts in the interests of the staff it handles, and you should not be offended if the agency discreetly checks you out. Bear in mind that as an employer, you have responsibilities too, all of which help promote a secure and fair working relationship. Sue recommends the following:

• Be realistic about wages—ask around to compare what is a reasonable wage for the hours and skills required.

• Don't employ untrained or unqualified staff (particularly au pairs) unless you intend to supervise and guide them in their duties.

- Always issue a contract of employment and agree to pay tax and National Insurance.
- Always negotiate wages net of tax and insurance.
- Make sure your household insurance covers liability for anyone you employ in your home—check specifically that you are covered if the nanny has an accident while working. Same goes for motor insurance, if she is driving your car. If she is driving her own, make sure her insurers know she is using it for work. If your nanny is a member of the Professional Association of Nursery Nurses (PANN), she will be covered by their free members-only insurance policy, otherwise you could contact one of the firms who specialise in arranging cover for nannies and mother's helps on her behalf (see addresses on page 204). If you intend to employ a temporary nanny through an agency ask if the agency has insurance to cover her. Many do not.

Although it by no means includes all the reputable agencies in the country, the Federation of Recruitment and Employment Services (FRES) can recommend a list of its members who specialise in supplying nannies and au pairs. All the agencies on this list have paid to join FRES, but before being admitted to the list they are personally checked out and the service they offer is investigated by FRES staff. Each member agency is expected to follow a nine-point Code of Good Recruitment Practice. Christine Little, who handles the nanny agency side, says that members can be expelled if evidence of malpractice is proven.

However, while an employment agency can have its licence revoked, no such scheme exists for individual nannies, particularly where cruelty or abuse is suspected but not proved. The head of one top London agency, who actually admitted she was too frightened to be named, reiterated the warning to parents to check back as far as they can and investigate any unexplained 'gaps' in employment history.

'Names can be changed, people can disappear and re-emerge several years later. We interviewed one nanny, a mature "Mary Poppins" type, who was absolutely charming. However, my intuition told me she was too good to be true. She had worked in America, and when I checked back I discovered she had been suspected of choking children—forcing objects down their throats and rushing them to hospital just in time to be hailed as hero of the hour. Incredibly, parents refused to believe the doctor's suspicions and she was never charged. I wouldn't have her on our books, of course, but I have since learnt that she has created a new identity and is still answering job advertisements, totally plausible and mad as a hatter.'

The Interview

The telephone is an important pre-selection tool—use it to winnow prospective interviewees to a manageable shortlist before you commit yourself to actually meeting them. Run through the job description with each caller—don't assume that all applicants, even from an agency, will have fully understood your requirements.

'Make sure they have actually noticed the age of your child and have experience of that age group,' recommends Alexandra Campbell, whose first choice of nanny lasted one week. Although a competent nanny, she just hadn't realised that looking after twin babies would restrict her other activities quite so much. 'A nanny who has grown used to the social whirl of outings and parties with other nannies and toddlers will find looking after tiny babies rather isolating,' points out Alexandra. 'It saves time and trouble to only see those with a real knowledge and affinity for tinies. When I started interviewing a second time, I immediately asked everyone who rang up "What is your favourite age to look after?". Even though I had clearly specified the age of my twins (three months) I heard several cheerful, "Oh, two to three year olds".'

The most efficient way of keeping track of all the various details is to keep a sheaf of standardised 'application forms' by the phone. This makes it easier to compare notes and has the added advantage of letting someone else take a call without missing the vital details. For example, you could quickly cover the following over the phone:

● Name, address, telephone number (find out if this is her own flat/live-in job/parents' house?)
● Age, training, experience.
● Ask for a brief description of her present job—basic details, number of kids and their ages, hours worked, type of duties. (You could also ask why she is leaving it or why she is interested in yours.)
● Fill in more details of your job—check she is still interested.
● Check when she will be available, that she can drive/owns her own car/doesn't smoke/can provide references.

Pull out the most promising candidates and fix interviews to last about an hour, with half an hour between to assess each one. Don't see too many people in one day or your recollections will blur. Interviewing takes up a lot of nervous energy, particularly when you are trying to make a good impression too. A day spent in concentrated character assessment can leave your intuition in shreds.

Having your child present at the interview

On balance, the arguments for having your child or children present, at least for some of the time, seems to win out.

The presence of children stops the whole proceedings from becoming too intimidating, and after all nanny is going to be spending more time with them than you. It's vital to see how they react together, allowing for shyness and nerves. But, depending on the age of your offspring, it's probably a good idea to have someone else on hand to remove them after a while if they become too distracting.

'What impressed me immediately about Antoinette was the way she was so natural with the children,' remembers Isobel McKenzie Price. 'She was genuinely interested in them, but she waited until they came to her. Then she focused her full attention on them, deciding if she really liked them too, which is just as important. And she didn't put on an act for my benefit, providing the slick and polished answers of an NNEB. I think the moment that clinched it was when I trotted out the "what would she give the children to eat?", and she looked up from playing with them and said "Whatever they like, really, it's pointless trying to force them!"'

The trick questions

Resist the temptation to fire off a salvo of these, even though you fear you are not getting through to the real person. Far better to have an apparently friendly, relaxed chat first about the job, during which time you can observe a candidate with your children. Ask her about her general experience and past history; cover the basic areas of how she would feed, entertain, and discipline your children, and probe a little deeper with some questions about her private life—if you phrase these carefully only the nanny with a great deal to hide will be evasive. 'I always ask about their social

life,' says Alexandra Campbell. 'It can tell you a great deal about
how a girl will conduct herself generally.' Isobel agrees. 'Find out
how much in control she is of her own life before letting her loose
in yours!'

By now, say experienced nanny interviewers, you will know in
your heart if she is Ms Right, but if you still feel you are being fed
the official line, liven up the proceedings with a few of the following
examples, where the answers will reveal more of the candidate's
personality:

- What do you like least about working with children?
- What would you do if . . . (insert disaster of your choice)
- Have you ever had to cope with a real emergency?
- What do you feel is the most important part of a nanny's job?
- An eagerly awaited special trip is rained off. What do you do
instead?
- Do you have a special skill or outside interests—e.g. swimming,
playing a musical instrument, dancing, foreign language?
- Do you see a lot of your family/are you close?/what do they
think of you being a nanny?
- What do you like to do to relax?
- Do you have a steady relationship at present?
- Do you have any strong religious beliefs?
- Are you a vegetarian/do you follow any kind of special diet?
- How would you counteract racist or sexist behaviour towards
my children, or observed by them, or even expressed by them?

Last but certainly not least, you should always ask why they are
leaving their previous job. Some nannies may concoct stories to
hide the almighty row they have had with a previous employer;
checking references will reveal the extent of their imagination/
duplicity/sense of humour. But a nanny who is honest enough to
admit she didn't like her employer, was badly treated, or was
simply undermined by her employer's attitude is giving you valuable clues, not least on how to avoid losing her the same way.
However, be prepared for some surprises! Experienced nanny
sharers Sue and Tessa thought they'd heard all the 'moving on'
excuses until one extremely promising, highly qualified and experienced candidate told them she left her last job 'because I fell in
love with my employer's husband and we ran away together. We
are now married.'

It helps to have a detailed written job description to hand, to
make you cover all that you expect your nanny to do. Tell her

about your work, and if you are regularly home late, be upfront
about this by explaining how much overtime/time off in lieu you
are prepared to offer. Discuss her hours, pay, perks, use of car,
tell her about the children's current activities and also what your
intended plans for them are, attending toddlers' gym, playgroup
etc. so she has a clear idea of how much running around there will
be. You could let the best candidates take away a copy to absorb
at leisure.

Checking References

**It is absolutely imperative that you check up on even the most
apparently admirable of candidates.** Don't let embarrassment or
even intimidation by a highly qualified and experienced nanny stop
you from thoroughly investigating their past—every good nanny
will expect you to. 'It's really weird how some parents seem happy
to rely just on qualifications and written references,' says one
nanny, who admitted that her opinion of an employer dropped if
they didn't seem willing to make the effort to protect their children
like this.

Despite some rather old-fashioned views that referees should
only be contacted by letter, far and away the best method of getting
to the truth is to use the phone, where applicants are soon damned
by faint praise. 'Just a tone of voice will speak volumes,' says
Alexandra Campbell, who remembers one distinctly 'off' referee
who seemed completely thrown to be contacted and without actually saying anything derogatory managed to convey that hiring that
particular candidate would be utter madness. 'You must always
listen between the lines!'

If your chosen candidate can't produce an NNEB certificate, the
board will verify they have passed if you contact them in writing
(see address on page 204). The board will supply up to two dupli-
cates for careless candidates, so don't believe those who say they've
mislaid their original and can't get another.

Some agencies now ask for a complete work history, and there's
no reason why you shouldn't ask for an experienced nanny's CV,
as any other kind of employer would. This will help if you want
to check further back, and it's reasonable to expect a nanny to
explain any long gaps in employment.

The Settling-in Period

The first few days or weeks can make or break a working relationship between mother and nanny. You will probably want to specify a trial period (six–eight weeks is standard) in the contract in case either of you has made a big mistake, but from day one start as you mean to go on by establishing a friendly but respectful employer/employee relationship. A sensitive nanny will expect a few ups and downs while you get back into the routine of work, but don't unnerve her completely by metamorphosing from chatty pal to haughty office queen.

Make the handover gradual; it's best if the nanny can start at least a week before you have to return to work so that you can show her the ropes while she and the children get to know each other in a relaxed way. 'The children have to get to know you from behind their mother's skirts, so to speak,' says Antoinette, who spent a week working together with Isobel. 'They have to see that she has faith in you and that she is happy and positive about the whole arrangement.'

The Working Relationship

Mutual respect, trust and sensitivity are the key to any good relationship. Joan, a 23-year-old NNEB-trained, experienced nanny, stresses good communication as the way of avoiding potential problems. 'You've got to see eye to eye—you are partners in bringing up a child.'

In her previous jobs, a more innocent Joan suffered varying degrees of exploitation and in one case, she was treated virtually 'as a household slave' by a domineering father. Now Joan demands the respect she deserves and her confidence has made her more of an equal with her present employer.

'We get on so well that I'm now a godmother to one of my charges. The mother and I often sit down together at the end of the day and have a chat over a glass of wine. She is always concerned to know that I am happy, and in return I try to be as sensitive as possible to her feelings, particularly those that a working mother finds hard to express. There was a time when she was working really long hours from 9 am until 10 pm and seeing very little of her child. He began to always run to me for comfort, even when she was there, which I could see upset her, although she didn't say anything. So I set up all sorts of activities that his mum could continue, to keep her involved.'

Caroline Bennion, an ex-nanny who married and now has a baby son of her own, remembers the not so little things which used to get to her.

'It seems petty, but at one job I would arrive every morning to find the sink stacked with dirty dishes from the night before. I had to either wash, or move everything before I could even start preparing food for the children. But more hurtful is the way some employers just dismiss your hard work by going on about their "terrible week" at the office and implying you've got the easier time of it. One woman I worked for drove me mad by ignoring me when she arrived home and instead asking her year-old baby "and what have you been doing today?"'

In contrast, Antoinette is full of praise for the way that her employer Isobel 'respects me as a person, somebody with feelings and moods. I have good and bad days and so does she—we can be ratty with each other without it being the end of the world. In fact, it's uncanny how alike we are, we share similar opinions about children, which is probably why we just "clicked" at first. Isobel appreciates what a difficult job it is to look after children properly and how much effort it takes; my previous employers expected me to keep an eye on their kids over the ironing board!'

In return for a proper contract, generous holidays and clearly defined overtime agreements, Antoinette is flexible about working late when required and Isobel gives plenty of time off in return. While Antoinette's duties are spelt out in her job description, she is happy to do useful jobs around the house without being asked.

'She'll take advantage of a nice sunny day to put the washing machine on, small things which are actually really useful,' explains Isobel. 'She knows I'd never take advantage and vice versa. Even after three years she is still scrupulous about asking permission to have someone else in the house—even her mum!—and she always asks before taking the children out anywhere. But we are relaxed in other ways—the big breakthrough came when we both yelled at the kids in front of each other. The girls call her "week mummy" and knowing that they are so happy with her means I can get on with my work with complete peace of mind. Her salary is twice my mortgage, but she's worth it. I wish I could afford to pay her even more.'

Problems With Partners

All your hard work building up a rapport with nanny is going to be wasted if your man starts muttering about how well paid she is to sit around all day drinking coffee. No one understands how hard it is to look after children until they have actually done it, so it pays dividends to make sure your man has had sole charge for a day and you are not likely to hear another peep out of him.

Successful Nanny Sharing

The secret is to share a similar outlook on life as well as a good nanny, say those with experience. Some say it is better to be friendly with the other mother and advertise and interview together, others that it's not really necessary, but all stress you must have the same views on fundamental aspects of childcare.

It's fine to jointly direct the nanny over areas like food, discipline and entertaining, but the best way to handle the business end of a nanny share is to appoint one mother as sole employer, who deals with pay and National Insurance. This avoids confusion and gives the nanny one person rather than a committee to deal with. It also means you can add more mothers and children to the share without hopelessly complicating the whole thing.

Sue, a social services manager, and Tessa, a television producer, are old hands at the nanny share game—they started out modestly sharing a nanny between them. Tessa now presides over a successful four-way share involving five children, two aged six, and a five, four and three year old!

Naturally it takes the right sort of nanny to handle this combination (and bear in mind that under the Children Act any nanny working for more than two families must be registered with the local authority). But because more mothers are involved the group can afford to employ an exceptional experienced and qualified nanny, Lisa, who is also an ex-children's entertainer.

Sue and Tessa met in a doctor's surgery while waiting for their antenatal appointments. They have kept up both their friendship and the arrangement for over five years; Sue thinks that sharing the responsibility as well as the cost is a real advantage, and the partnership has weathered several unsuitable nannies and sharers.

They have an enviably relaxed attitude as expressed by Sue: 'After so long, we don't panic if a nanny leaves—or even if we have to sack one. We just stick another ad in *The Lady*, very straightforward, giving hours, pay and the number of children. Also, having four mums involved means there is far more flexibility if a nanny is sick—someone can usually take time off.'

How it works

At present Tessa, who has the largest house, plays host to children and nanny and shoulders the extra costs of heating and lighting. Her husband Tim is a financial wizard, so he has always handled the tax and National Insurance. All other sharers split the food bill between them.

Each mother in the share pays per number of 'child hours' she uses. All mothers take their children to school or nursery, so nanny Lisa is not required to clock on until 11.30 am during term time, when she collects the youngest child from nursery. On most days she then has this child alone until she picks up the other children from school at 3.30 pm and brings them home for tea, fun and games until parents start arriving around 6 pm. During holidays, when she has all the children full time, Lisa has agreed to forego extra payment in favour of extra weeks holiday. Tessa and her husband usually have the whole month of August off, so the other sharers fall in with this.

Tessa and Sue say they now have their double act down to a fine art when interviewing a nanny. Each has different priorities in a nanny so they take it in turns to cover various areas. Once they have made a choice, the other mums then meet the candidate separately to 'rubber stamp' the decision.

'As long as you can rely on the other mothers to take their responsibilities seriously, paying and dropping children on time, the share will work. But it's important to make sure the children are all getting on well, and that by adding another you are not upsetting the balance.'

A four-way share may seem rather ambitious at first, but gets easier as children grow older and benefit from lively company. The permutations are many and various and can operate for part of the

day, week, or even year. For example, you could share a nanny
with a teacher during term time and replace her child with another
during the long summer break, or, if you only want a nanny for
pre- and post-school times, you could 'piggy back' another local
full-time nanny (see Chapter 7). Another option, although
uncommon, has certainly worked for Sian Stephens, who 'shares'
her nanny with another child!

Sian's nanny has a baby the same age as her son Sam, and for a
corresponding reduction in salary she brings him to work with her
every day. 'We thoroughly discussed the possibility that she would
favour her own child, but we decided to give it a try, because we
liked her so much,' says Sian. 'Everything has worked out fine—I
have a highly professional carer for what is an affordable amount
for me, Sam has a pal of his own age and my nanny, a single
mother, has a job.'

CHAPTER 6

Nurseries: The Good, the Bad and the Ugly

Full day nursery care is so scarce in this country that many working mothers cannot be blamed for regarding it as more of a dream than a real option in their choice of childcare. Currently there is nursery provision for less than 2% of children aged up to four, while surveys show that more than one in five parents would prefer to send their child to a nursery rather than use a childminder or nanny. However, the good news is that in the private sector the situation is slowly improving as new businesses respond to the challenge of providing full day group care, many in partnership with public sector organisations. Employers are now more receptive to the idea of workplace nurseries, too.

Many harassed working mothers favour the idea (or rather the ideal!) of a nursery because it puts childcare on a more obviously professional and less personal footing. While it is important to develop a positive and friendly relationship with nursery staff, you don't have to suffer the sagas of their private lives. Not for you the childcare crisis when your two-timed nanny takes to her bed in paroxysms of grief, or when the childminder's mother-in-law throws another wobbly. Nurseries take a lot of the unpredictability out of childcare arrangements, although they do have other drawbacks for working mothers.

For obvious reasons, most research into daycare has tended to concentrate on the 'public' domain of the nursery rather than the more private and inaccessible worlds of childminder or nanny, so at present there is no reliable comparative evidence available. But there is much reassuring research available to the effect that the child who attends a well-run, high-quality nursery benefits both socially and intellectually, and performs better in a variety of subjects later at school.

However, there are a number of dissenting voices about the effects on babies and very young children; American researcher Jan Belsky claims to have found that children who start full daycare under one year old were at risk of forming an insecure attachment to their mothers.

Belsky's results were based on the effects of American daycare, which is largely unregulated and often of frighteningly poor quality. Also, his work has been criticised both here and in America because of his controversial testing methods. But the research makes valid points about staffing ratios for babies, who need to relate to one, trusted adult. The high staff turnover in some nurseries could jeopardise a baby's ability to develop a secure relationship. Few British working mothers will have the option of a nursery place for a tiny baby, but if you do there are extra factors to bear in mind (see Babies in Daycare, below).

Naturally there are pros and cons to be weighed up first, and you must apply the same rigorous 'inspection and selection' procedure that you would with any other form of daycare. This chapter will help you decide your priorities, and provides a comprehensive check list to assist in your choice of nursery. It applies mainly to private day nurseries, but even if you are offered a place at a workplace or community nursery you will need to satisfy yourself that it offers good quality care.

Do not be lulled into a false sense of security because you know that all nurseries have to be inspected and approved by Social Services, or because you have physical proof that so many other parents are willing to leave their child there! You have to take into account your own child's personality and needs, which will be better served by some styles of nursery than others, however praiseworthy the basic standards of care.

Also, you must consider your needs too. Nurseries are the least flexible form of daycare in terms of hours. While most open strictly 8 am–6 pm (with some workplace nurseries slightly longer), your own working day may be a lot more erratic. A nanny, or to a lesser extent a childminder, who doesn't 'shut up shop on the dot', is a better choice if you constantly have to stay late. And think twice before committing yourself to rising an hour earlier each morning in order to manage your journey to work, via that wonderful new nursery located on the other side of town!

ADVANTAGES OF GROUP DAYCARE

- Nurseries are 100% reliable (short of fire or flood!); open all year round, apart from Bank Holidays and Christmas.
- Subsidised nurseries (see below) can be the least expensive form of childcare.
- Your child can enjoy the company of a wide range of children of different ages and cultural backgrounds. Research shows that the rich social life of the nursery helps promote independence and confidence.
- In relating to several members of staff rather than just one carer, your child is able to develop a variety of relationships with adults.
- Nurseries provide a wide range of toys, activities, facilities for indoor and outdoor play, far greater than a childminder or nanny could provide.

DISADVANTAGES

- Nurseries are not flexible about opening times—this may cause nightmarish juggling if your working pattern is erratic.
- Some private nurseries can be extremely expensive, and not all offer discounts for siblings.
- Location: the best nursery may be hell to get to every morning, or be in the opposite direction from your work.
- Illness spreads like wildfire and a sick child will have to be cared for at home by you or an alternative carer. Bear in mind too that you are at risk of picking up the bugs too, thus losing more time off work!
- Lack of places for under-twos.

You and Your Child: Changing Needs

At present, a nursery is unlikely to be your first choice of care for your baby. Local authority nurseries will take children from birth to four years, but restricted places mean they are not usually an option for a working mother. The high staff/children ratio, extra equipment and tighter regulations on space mean that only a few private nurseries will take children under two, as it is far more expensive for them to provide places.

Finding a place from the end of your maternity leave will be very difficult, particularly if you are returning to work after three months. Many working mothers prefer the more personal, home-based care of nannies or childminders for tiny babies anyway. But after the age of two, nearly every child will benefit from a more challenging, social environment. You can arrange a 'cocktail' of childcare to accommodate this, possibly combining a nanny or childminder to take your child to and from part-time nursery classes. But long waiting lists exist for many full-time nurseries, so if you are keen on your child getting a future place, it's worth putting your name down as early as possible and finding alternative care for the first two years.

Ideally, your one carefully chosen carer will provide continuity of care until your child no longer needs it. Chapter 4 illustrated the virtues of a trained childminder who changes and 'grows' with your children, adapting her care to provide some early education and plenty of social contact. But it has to be said that some child-minders are brilliant with babies and toddlers, but don't cope with older children so well. The same is true of some nannies, who are a more transient species generally. Realistically, the shortage of good childcare generally means that many working mothers make the best choice they can at the time.

Remember, too, that circumstances change—what may have been a sound choice for your infant may no longer be as suitable for your lively two year old, as happened to one *SHE* reader: 'When my son first started at his minder at six months, she also looked after two other little ones and everyone was happy with this arrangement. Gradually, the other children left for various reasons and were not replaced. By the time he was two, my son was getting one-to-one care at a price other mothers envied, but he wasn't mixing with any other children his age. I felt the minder was gradually losing interest in going out. I began to feel he wasn't being stimulated enough during the day; he started playing up at bedtime, wanting more and more attention. I was determined he should meet more children, so I tried a fresh approach and found a nursery place.'

For another mother, moving her daughter from childminder to nursery was as much for her benefit as her child's: 'It sounds horrid, but I felt the emotional input required was wearing me out. Looking back it was my fault; I became so afraid of upsetting my child-minder that I was too nice, too accommodating. I practically became an agony aunt, and to be honest, I have enough problems with my own family. She was wonderful with my daughter Susie (who was 20 months) and I had no complaints about her care, but she was a worrier, prophesying the worst whenever Susie had the slightest cough or cold. It began to get me down. When several of my friends started their children at a new private local nursery it sounded like bliss—to be greeted with a smile by friendly, enthusiastic staff rather than another tale of doom and gloom. Susie got a place after a couple of months and is absolutely loving it. As for me, I feel a new woman!'

What is Available?

In the UK, day nurseries fall into four main categories:

Local Authority Nurseries: run by Social Services with admission usually limited to children deemed to be 'at risk', although some local authorities do have wider admission criteria. They are open to children aged from birth to four years, and charges are generally low for all-day care, all year round. If you are a single working mother it is probably worth enquiring, as every avenue should be explored, but don't get your hopes up.

Community Nurseries: run by community groups of voluntary organisations, and registered with Social Services. Usually only cater for children aged two–five. There is much emphasis on parental involvement, which often includes helping out at sessions as well as fund raising, so they are really more suitable for part-time working mums. Opening hours are generally 8 am–6 pm all year round with short breaks, and charges are generally low, so places are much in demand.

Workplace Nurseries: set up by employers on or off site, and they usually cater for children from birth to five years, although places are often limited for babies, despite high demand as mothers return to work earlier. Some cater for employees from different companies who 'buy' places for their staff. Pressure from working parents has persuaded many employers to start up nurseries, but they are not suitable for all types of workplace, particularly those in the inner city. Good points include being physically near to your child (breastfeeding mums can continue through their lunchhour!). The main disadvantages are that children may have to travel long distances daily in rush hour traffic or public transport. If you change jobs, you lose your place, and in some companies, places are restricted to senior staff. Opening hours usually cover a normal working day, but there are a few workplace nurseries which are geared to shift workers. Charges vary, but are usually subsidised by the employer.

Private Day Nurseries: with no admission criteria other than ability to pay the fee, private nurseries provide the most realistic option for the working parent of children aged two–five. As with other day nurseries, these must be registered with Social Services and meet the standards laid down in the Children Act 1989. Apart from satisfying official criteria, standards can vary tremendously between nurseries. Approach with caution! Some call themselves 'nursery schools' which can mean one of two things: a) they think it makes them sound better, or b) the person in charge may have a nursery education qualification and can offer a more specifically educational approach. Opening hours are usually 8 am–6 pm, and charges are relatively high, anywhere from £70 to over £100 per week.

How to Find Your Ideal Nursery

Nurseries themselves are easy enough to spot—it's the places which can be difficult to track down. But don't let warnings of a waiting list deter you; for reasons known only to nursery managers themselves lists can sometimes mysteriously be juggled and suddenly you have a place much sooner than you anticipated. Don't ask questions—just accept with alacrity!

All types of nurseries listed above must be registered with the Social Services department, so ask for a copy of the local list. If you are lucky enough to have a large and bewildering choice, pare it down by first cutting out all nurseries which are more than a short drive away. (Be firm, you can always extend your 'boundaries' later.) At this stage your choice will be guided by your feelings about child development. Is it important to you that your child receives specifically educational care, for example Montessori? Or would she be happier in a more unstructured, 'learn through play' environment?

Send for the prospectuses which interest you and cast a critical eye over the information, particularly if the nursery has 'school' in the title. You will need to know much more about the teaching qualifications of the staff. Remember that a prospectus for a private nursery has much in common with a holiday brochure when it comes to flatteringly pretty pictures, but at least with a nursery you can 'see before you buy'. Once you've picked three or four possibles, it's time to get tough. Make an appointment, and take your child with you if possible for the first visit, which should last at least half an hour.

Karen and Joe, both teachers, used a childminder for their daughter Rebecca when Karen went back to work. Rebecca, born prematurely, was still small and rather fragile, so the warm, motherly care of the minder was ideal. But by the time Rebecca was two, she was ready for more stimulating activities, including more practical and 'messy' play which the childminder couldn't provide.

They looked at several local day nurseries, but were most impressed by a small, purpose-built new nursery which offered lots of activities rather than set 'lessons'. Neither of them wanted a specifically educational approach, but were pleased to hear that the nursery provided increasing amounts of learning through play as the children developed.

'I was particularly impressed by how keen the staff were to please,' remembers Karen. 'As a new nursery they were open to suggestions from parents—I felt they welcomed ideas. The cultural mix of children reflected the ethnic diversity of the area, which meant that Rebecca would benefit from a wider circle of friends. The nursery made a lot of effort to be multi-cultural—the menus reflected this and I remember all the children had made lanterns to celebrate the Chinese New Year.'

Karen used the Easter holidays to settle Rebecca into the nursery, which meant she could spend more time with her. This helped Rebecca, and meant that Karen could see a day's activities for herself. Apart from being reassured further, this also makes a link between them, as Karen has first-hand knowledge of how her daughter is spending the day.

Rebecca is enjoying herself tremendously; both Joe and Karen are so pleased with her progress that they plan to leave her at the nursery until she starts school. 'The amount of formal learning gradually increases as the children grow older,' explains Joe. 'At three they are starting to learn letters—she can already recognise her name and those of her best friends. The staff/child ratio is far better than anything Rebecca would experience in a state nursery class, and while those classes are free, we would still have to find and pay for "fill in" childcare.'

BABIES IN DAYCARE

The care of babies is far more intensive, time-consuming and requires a completely different approach. There is conflicting evidence on the effects of institutional daycare on babies, but most experts agree on the basics of good quality care for very young children. Check the following:

- Official staffing ratios should be 3:1, some dedicated nursery managers increase this to 2:1. Ask if the nursery operates a 'key worker' system, where each baby is assigned a regular member of staff who becomes her main carer. Even the tiniest baby needs to build a relationship with one trusted adult rather than be confronted with a variety of caregivers.
- Ask about staff turnover—it's even more important not to have constant changes where babies are concerned.
- Babies must be in a separate room, away from the noise and bustle of older children.
- At feeding times, do adults hold the babies, talk to them and look at them while giving bottles? Are there lots of cuddles?
- Babies need a variety of stimulating textures in their play things and safe, interesting surfaces to crawl over.

What to Look for When Choosing a Nursery

Despite sensible guidelines in the 1989 Children Act, there is no standard 'measure' of the quality of daycare in Britain. At present, local authorities have to interpret the basic tenets of the Act themselves when inspecting daycare providers under their control. Over the next three years, researchers from the Thomas Coram Institute will be working on a major project to establish a British measure of quality which can be widely used to assess daycare in this country. Until then, parents will have to judge each nursery for themselves, but there are certain obvious 'signs' of good quality care (see below), regardless of whether the nursery is housed in a gleaming new block or an old church hall.

It really helps to have your child with you on a first visit, because not only do you need her reaction to the nursery, you need to see how the staff respond to her. After soaking up the general atmosphere you can return alone on a subsequent visit if you want to ask the staff more questions. The following is a checklist of things to watch out for when visiting a nursery.

1. Are the children happy?

Do they appear content and involved in play? This is perhaps the most important test of all. Allowing for some minor skirmishes and grizzling, on the whole children should be engrossed in activity. An open plan room with 'unstructured' activity where the children can choose what to do, needs careful organisation from the staff or it can disintegrate into chaos.

GOOD SIGNS: Happy, absorbed, busy children. A certain noise level, neither an unnatural hush (could indicate a great deal of repression) nor an unpleasant hubbub (lack of control). Children playing together and helping each other, if appropriate to their age.

BAD SIGNS: Children wandering aimlessly, fighting, crying, sitting in trances (all indicate boredom, insufficient space, lack of play equipment or structure to the session).

2. How do the staff relate to the children?

Does it seem that enough warm, individual attention is given to each child? Do staff appear enthusiastic? (Bear in mind that some will be much better with children than adults, particularly younger members of staff who may find you a bit overwhelming at first. Watch them with the children, rather than be put off by appearance or monosyllabic replies to your questions.) Do staff members help build self confidence by praising and encouraging? Do they give the children choices and help them to be independent?

GOOD SIGNS: Children talking to adults, adults listening carefully and giving considered replies. Adults talking to babies as well as older children. Staff who get down physically to children's level; who spend a lot of time sitting on the floor and who obviously enjoy giving children a cuddle. Staff who can resolve conflict firmly without screaming or shouting.

BAD SIGNS: overworked, harassed staff. Unobservant adults, who don't address children by name or listen properly. Children who don't look up at adults or address them regularly. Staff who are always smartly dressed and crumple-free!

3. Is there a plentiful supply of safe, good quality play equipment and plenty of activities to choose from?

Look for a) messy play—water and sand b) quiet, independent play—books, jigsaws, puzzles c) social play—dressing-up clothes, household objects, dolls, puppets, musical instruments d) creative play—paints, clay, dough, crayons, beads, paper e) outdoor play —climbing frame, slides, bikes, pushing toys. If the nursery does take babies, are there plenty of soft, cuddly toys and objects of varying textures to provide interest? Do toys and books reflect multi-cultural influences and present positive images of black people?

4. How is the space organised?

There should be quiet areas and noisy, social spaces. Some American research seems to suggest that children are more attentive and responsive if a nursery is divided into small rooms, but this isn't always possible. However, even a church hall can be sectioned off with imaginative use of folding partitions or curtains to avoid presenting a crowded, monotonous space.

5. How is the nursery decorated and furnished?

GOOD SIGNS: Lots of work displayed, bright decorations at children's level, low shelves so they can reach their toys and books themselves, high cupboards for safe storage of materials. Furniture which is child sized—low tables and chairs. Windows low enough to let children see outside. Child-sized lavatories and basins. If the nursery is having to 'make do' in a rather dingy church hall, look at the efforts made to cheer it up.

BAD SIGNS: Wreckage, broken toys, mess from the previous day left untouched. Little evidence of work displayed. Carelessly stored materials or wasted materials.

6. How is discipline and supervision handled?

Do staff supervise without constantly intruding on solitary or social play? Some disputes are inevitable and older children learn from them to share and negotiate. But what happens during episodes of biting, scratching? How do staff cope? Plus, are there few rules in evidence, which are vital for safe and secure play, e.g. no loud screaming or shouting, no throwing sand or water, only one on the slide at a time?

7. How are mealtimes organised?

Is the food good and varied? Are meals served at reasonable times
and on schedule? Does the cooking take account of different cultural backgrounds? If there are babies, do adults hold them and
talk to them while giving them bottles? Do all children eat together?
(Ask yourself if you would enjoy eating at this place.)
GOOD SIGNS: Menu for the week pinned up, showing multi-cultural
dishes. Proper tables and chairs. Meals treated as a social event,
conversation encouraged. Clean kitchen. Sensitivity to dietary
needs, good knowledge of wholefood, restricted sugar, avoiding
additives etc.
BAD SIGNS: No menu on show, haphazard timings for lunch. Over
repressive atmosphere during mealtimes.

8. Is there a quiet room for sleep/napping? How are the children encouraged to sleep? Do younger ones have proper cots?

GOOD SIGNS: A well-ventilated, quiet room. Staff member who
asks about child's idiosyncrasies, e.g. 'does she like having her face
stroked to get her off to sleep?'
BAD SIGNS: A crowded, stuffy room. Rigidly timetabled nap times
with little interest shown in children's personal preferences.

9. Hygiene and safety

Don't forget to observe the basic safety requirements, as Social
Services may not have visited for quite a while. Is the outside door
always shut to prevent escapees and to deter intruders? Are stairs
gated? Are all heaters and power points protected? Is all equipment
clean and well maintained? Are there enough fire appliances? Are
lavatories and kitchens clean and safe?

Also, look at the general cleanliness of the children. A balanced
approach is most desirable, i.e. dirty play is fine, but there should
be a cleaning up session afterwards. Are hands and faces washed
after lunch. Are the children tidied up for hometime? Bad signs
are extremes either way—obsessive cleanliness or toddlers running
round with sagging nappies.

Questions to Ask When Choosing a Nursery

Be brazen and take a list with you if it helps. The way staff respond should tell you a lot—especially about their feelings on parental involvement! If you've previously blanched at grilling childminders on their home territory, you should find the less intimate nursery setting far more conducive. Remember to check the practical details like:

• Opening hours, holidays and fees payable (are there any increases pending?)

• Staff qualifications: you are fully entitled to ask about training and experience, particularly if the nursery has 'school' in its title. Staff may be nursery nurses, teachers, nurses or playleaders, and some may be students.

• Does your child need to be prepared in any way, e.g. out of nappies, able to feed herself?

• What are the procedures for emergencies? Is there sufficient first-aid equipment?

Once you've covered the basics, move on to the nursery manager's approach to child development. As with any carer, it's vital that you share a similar philosophy. Some nurseries promote orderliness and manners, others free expression, some carefree exploration, others intense learning. Ask the manager what she considers is the most important aspect in the care of babies and young children. (Interpret a blank look as a very bad sign indeed!)

• What actually happens throughout the day? You may encounter two quite different types of approach, one is the 'totally unstructured' session, where children have totally free choice. There is no set time for breaks, stories or music, and children move from one activity to the next. It needs an extremely gifted teacher or supervisor to prevent this freedom developing into chaos. A more popular and workable alternative is the split session, where children have some free play and make choices, but this is combined with more structured activity where children will have a story together, or drama, or games, plus scheduled spaces for different activities. Children take regular breaks together. If the nursery is offering a more specifically educational approach you will want to know how this is organised for different ages.

• Daycare means sharing the care of your child with other people. Try to discover how much parental involvement is encouraged.

a) Are you given the chance to talk about changes in arrangements, coming events and activities?
b) What opportunities will you have to talk over your child's progress, or to tackle any problems?
c) How do they handle settling in? Are you encouraged to stay with your child if you wish?

By now you may be feeling that you will need to book an overnight stay at the nursery in order to observe and ask enough! But generally speaking, you will find that good things in childcare tend to go together. If you immediately notice that the relationships between adults and children are warm and friendly and the play materials varied and interesting, it's a pretty safe bet to expect that the kitchens are clean, the food nutritious and the activities stimulating and well organised. Likewise if you meet overworked adults and see few play materials, the meals are likely to be poor and the children bored, unhappy or out of control.

Sue, a refugee liaison teacher, has both her daughters Hannah, 14 months, and Louisa, three, at the same nursery. Sue and her husband Alan, a solicitor, have found that this is still less expensive than a daily nanny. Another important plus for Sue is that she escapes the hassle of catering for children and nanny.

'I just love not having to think about food! When Louisa was at a childminder's I had to provide most of it, and I think the childminder gave her too many sweets. Now I don't have to worry about them having fresh wholesome food. I drop them off on the dot of eight, just as the nursery opens, and breakfast is ready. They have a good lunch and tea, plus snacks and juice during the day. Every morning the toys are laid out—everything always looks fresh and exciting.'

Sue immediately liked the warm and caring atmosphere of the nursery when she first looked round, particularly in the 'baby' room for the under-twos. She was impressed by the obvious efforts to adopt a multi-cultural approach, and by the answers she received when talking to the nursery manager. 'She told me "I'm not having anyone shouting at these children". There are lots of cuddles—someone always has a child on their hip!—and so far there hasn't been a single change of staff. I am always made to feel welcome when I stop for a chat in the evening—someone has time to tell me how the two girls have been that day.'

Settling Your Child Into Nursery

Even if your child has previously been used to being left with a childminder or nanny, it's a big step to have to cope with a group of children, different adults and a noisier, more bustling environment altogether. It's worth taking some time off if possible so that the process isn't rushed and you can stay with your child, although you may find yourself waved away by a confident little hand on the second day!

Find out what your child will need to bring (a change of clothes almost certainly, possibly a painting shirt, a hand towel) so she is fully prepared. Don't dress her in best clothes, tempting though it may be. Power dressing is a purely adult way of confidence building! Older children don't want the added worry of having to keep clean all day.

She may want to take a favourite toy for comfort, but check with the nursery—this can cause problems. If your child has a blanket or comforter let her take it and hang it up with her coat, as it will make her feel better just knowing it is there. If she becomes really distressed she can cuddle it until you get there.

At first, it will help to play with her using the toys and apparatus available. Other children will inevitably become interested and want to join in, so use the opportunity to introduce your child to her potential playmates. After a while leave her free to wander about, but don't go out of her sight. She should be aware that you are still around to return to. It can be fascinating to watch your child in this new situation, but if you're twitching a bit ask nursery staff if there is some task you can do to help—cutting up paper, or tidying up.

How long you stay really depends on your child. If she seems happily settled leave her for a short time. Suggest to staff that you ring up in a couple of hours to see how things are going—you may not be needed after all!

Saying Goodbye Without (Too Many!) Tears

- Do be prepared to stay with your child until she is familiar with the environment.
- Always tell your child when you are going to leave. Never 'slip

away' to avoid tears when she is absorbed in play—this is really frightening for her and will shake her trust in you.

● Try hard to make your goodbye as bright and cheerful as you can, even if you're feeling really wobbly inside. Even with a very young child it's never a good idea to voice your misgivings in front of them.

● Make sure she has someone and something to distract her. Good nursery staff can be relied on to give her a cuddle and produce something 'exciting' to play with. It will help to encourage a special relationship between one or two of the staff so that she is always 'handed over' to the same person each day. This helps foster a sense of security.

● Set a time limit when you first leave, and give your child some idea of when you will return. 'See you in half an hour' is meaningless; try something like 'I'll be back after you've had lunch'.

Remember that most children settle happily and readily into nursery. Provided that you have chosen carefully, and spent a little time preparing your child for the change from home-based to nursery care, she will welcome this change to explore the beginnings of independence. Many parents speak delightedly of the rapid development of their children, socially and intellectually, once they start at a nursery. Seeing your child so obviously thriving, making friends and enjoying new challenges tends to reduce guilt feelings, particularly if you've experienced problems with previous care arrangements. There's another hidden bonus too—you don't have to wait until your child is at school before meeting lots of other mothers. And at a nursery for working parents and their children, you're going to meet a lot of like-minded women!

CHAPTER 7

Bridging the Gap—After-School and Holiday Care

Many working mothers of the under-fives, preoccupied with the problems of finding and maintaining full-time childcare, can be forgiven for adopting the 'Scarlett O'Hara' approach to future out-of-school care. 'I'll think about it tomorrow' is an understandable reaction from those who feel they have enough to cope with right now. When nanny has just resigned or the childminder's kids get chicken-pox, you may be forgiven for imagining that your troubles will be over once your kids are safely ensconced in 'big school'.

Unfortunately, it is then that they really begin! The earlier you can start investigating the options for bridging the gap between the end of school day and your working day (not to mention the yawning chasm of school holidays) the better. You may feel faintly ridiculous asking about after-school clubs or holiday camps for your babe in arms, but the sooner you have a clear picture of what is, or isn't available in your area the more time you will have to do something about it.

Finding appropriate and affordable childcare is no easier once children start school; in fact you are presented with a whole new set of problems. There is very little formal care provision for school age children; out-of-school schemes cater for only 0.2% of primary school children, holiday schemes for 0.3%. In real terms that means there are only around 400 out-of-school schemes, or 'kids' clubs', in the whole of the UK and most are in the major cities. At present most working parents have to survive on a day-to-day patchwork of informal arrangements. Good quality, reliable organised schemes would benefit both working parents and their children, but the Kids' Club Network, the only national organisation involved in over-five care, estimate that 25,000 out-of-school schemes are needed to meet demand.

If you are returning to work after a break and looking for term-time and holiday childcare you need solutions now, and there are

a variety of helpful suggestions below. Even if your child is a long
way off school age, you will still find this chapter very useful for
forward planning. There is plenty of groundwork you can do now
to smooth your way in the future, e.g. building up your local
network of mothers and neighbours, or lending your support to
an emerging out-of-school club. (See below for more information.)

The good news for mums looking for out-of-school care from
now on is that the 1989 Children Act, which came into force in
October 1991, requires that all childcare providers catering for
children *up to age eight* are registered with the local authority,
rather than age five, as previously. This means that after-school
clubs, holiday schemes and day camps, both council and privately
run, now come under official scrutiny. Local authorities have a
duty to regularly inspect and review these services, and hopefully
increase provision to meet demand. Local authorities are also duty-
bound to collate and publish details of all existing childcare provision in the area, so parents should benefit from a far more
co-ordinated and positive approach to services, and more readily
available and up-to-date information.

The suggestions in this chapter cover both day-to-day term-time
arrangements, plus suggestions for holiday care. You may find that
part-time care before and after school, often informally organised,
cannot be extended to provide full day care during the holidays.
Although there are after-school schemes which also provide full-
time holiday care, these are few and far between. More usually,
longer breaks will require a different set of arrangements. The two
areas are therefore dealt with separately below, with some ideas
for term-time emergencies (teachers' strikes, heating breakdown
etc.).

There is also the option of letting older, responsible children
come home alone. This is not a decision to be taken lightly, of
course, but is sometimes unavoidable. There is a lot you can do to
ensure in-home safety and sensible behaviour, and the 'Home
Alone?' checklist on page 109 is a useful guide in helping to ascer-
tain whether your children are mature enough to cope. There is
also advice and encouragement on setting up an after-school
scheme with other parents, and examples from working mothers
who have done it.

A Word About Schools

If you do have a choice in your area, your main concern will, naturally, be the standard of the schools in question. Ease of journey is likely to be fairly high on your list, too, but it's also a good idea to investigate the attitudes of headteachers and school governors towards working mothers. Be warned, there are still some headmasters who think that a mother's place is at the school gate prompt at 9 am and 3.30 pm, and while your child's education is paramount, think twice before subjecting yourself to six years' worth of black marks. Check whether the staff are receptive to ideas for using the school premises for out-of-hours kids' clubs, for example, or has any previous attempt to broach the subject met strong resistance? Does the school make an effort to help by being flexible about hours, say by opening earlier than normal? (Many schools now accept children up to 25 minutes early—a few make use of kitchen staff to offer breakfast, too.)

Helping your child settle in

Many children who have been used to full-time care, particularly with a lively childminder or at a busy nursery, regard starting school as exciting and adapt to the change well. More nervous types, or those children who have been at home with mum during pre-school years, will need more help and support to settle in. It can be tough if you have just started in a new job yourself, but be prepared to start work a little later for a few days so that you can take your child to school, then wait with her and chat, particularly if she doesn't know any other children. Or leave work early so you can be part of the school gate crowd for a few precious days—a great way of getting to know other mothers—as well as being able to hear all about your child's first few days.

Best of all (if the school encourages it), take a week's holiday from work and get involved with day-to-day school activities, perhaps helping with reading or assisting a teacher with practical work. This way you can get to know some of the teachers (make an impression on the head, if possible!), the layout and general routine of the school. This can provide a great link between you and your child as you will understand more of what she tells you about her day. Getting involved will also register you in the minds of teachers as a committed mother, and will possibly stand you in good stead later.

Day-to-Day Term-Time Care

If you or your partner has flexible working hours, you may be able to cope with the routine of taking and collecting yourselves, particularly if your child's school opens early. Without doubt this is the ideal arrangement, and it's worth trying to work out something between the two of you or, alternatively, try to alter your working hours slightly. However, for many working mothers who have to put in a longer day (or have a long journey to work) this isn't possible. Other informal options include:

A local mum who walks her children to the same school daily. She may be willing to pick up your child in the morning, and keep her at home for a couple of hours after school. If this is for less than two hours a day, or your child is over eight, she will not have to register as a childminder, but you should insist on giving her money as you will find it hard to repay her in other ways. Living under constant obligation can be very wearing. Spread word at school that you are looking for an unofficial 'minder', or pin a note on the school notice board.

Alternatively, if you work part time, you could try organising a small 'team' of other part-time mums who work complementary hours, so that one of you is always available to pick up and collect all the children one day a week, or to deal with a sick child, other emergency, etc. Your local branch of the Working Mothers Association may be able to put you in touch with other members wishing to join such a scheme.

A neighbour with children is ideal if they all go to the same school, but not an answer to the transport problem otherwise. However, you could drop your kids off next door to wait for the school run rota to pick them up while you dash off to work. Likewise, the rota could drop them off with your neighbour after school until you return. This probably works best with older children who can quietly watch television or get on with homework—it's not really fair to expect your neighbour to entertain them. Again, a commercial basis to this arrangement may keep it running more smoothly, particularly as you'll want your children to have some sort of snack and a drink to keep them going.

A school run rota is a good solution if it's only the journey which is causing problems. You can either join or organise a rota. The more the merrier—the beauty of a large team of parents is that your turn comes up very infrequently. If you can share the duty with your partner you may find you only need to be late for work once every two weeks or so—which most employers would find acceptable. Ask at school whether you are on anyone's route, pin up a note on the school board or ask to join an existing rota. Even if you could never take a turn during the week, you may be able to join an existing rota by offering your services as chauffeur at other unpopular times—Saturday morning dance or music classes, for example, or a weekend football or hockey match.

Responsible teenagers. If recommended highly by other parents and teachers, a sensible young person could be trusted to pick up your child from school and look after her at home until you arrive. In return for a babysitting fee, she could make tea and keep an eye on your child while getting on with some homework. Another plus is you have an ideal babysitter for evening engagements too!

Children join you at work. This is only really an option if you work near the school and possess the winning combination of well-behaved older children, a definite end to your working day and a sympathetic employer. I used to work with a resourceful single mother who had somehow wangled a parking space at our central London office. After accompanying her to work, her two children then had a short, safe tube journey to school and each evening they would discreetly appear at the back of the office until she was ready to leave. (This turned out to be far less disruptive than the frequent and highly entertaining 'check-in' phonecalls which ensued once they started going home alone!)

Employing an after-school carer

Childminder. Some childminders take children part time, both before and after school and during holidays. Expect to pay more per hour than the full-time rate. The new rules governing childminders under the Children Act now extend to cover the under-eights, so after-school places for this age group will be limited. There are no restrictions on older children, although you will need to be reassured that hordes of rowdy nine and ten year olds do not descend come 4 pm.

If you previously used a minder for your pre-school child you may be able to continue part time if she is willing, but this may mean she loses out financially. Other minders adore the baby/ toddler stage and are not so good at handling older children once they become more challenging. If you are interviewing after-school minders, see Chapter 5 for general things to ask. Other points to check are: how much experience has she had with older children? How would she cope with 'school problems' (can she listen, reassure, offer sensible advice)? Is there a quiet place for children to do homework?

Contact your local Social Services department for a list of registered minders, or advertise locally yourself (check that applicants are registered and ask for references). Minders often advertise themselves, in local foodstores or newsagents, particularly if they have part-time 'slots' that they want to fill.

Borrow a nanny. While it is not economically viable to retain your full-time nanny, you might be able to 'borrow' one for a short time each day. Ros Weatherall, a statistician from south London, approached a nearby friend who employed a full-time nanny for her baby. She agreed to let the nanny walk the baby down to school, pick up Ros's two children and return to their house for a couple of hours each day. The nanny went off duty when Ros returned, and the other mother came to collect her baby at the end of her working day.

Au pair. If you have a room to spare and a fairly relaxed household, you may find an au pair is an ideal solution once your children are at school. Even an au pair previously inexperienced with children can soon be trusted to cope for the two to three hours each day after school; after her bit of 'light' housework she'll have the rest of the day free for language classes and socialising. One or two nights' babysitting a week are also par for the course.

During school holidays you could rearrange her hours so that she is available full time for certain days and has other days completely free. You will need to combine her care with another holiday option, such as a 'treasure' (see below). See Chapter 5 for more information on finding and interviewing au pairs.

'Treasures'. A part-time mother's help, perhaps an older person from the neighbourhood, whom you pay to collect your child from school and make him or her tea, and perhaps prepare your supper and do a bit of ironing while she's there! She may also be able to fill some holiday gaps, too. She doesn't have to register with the Social Services because she comes into your home. You could find someone suitable by advertising in local shop windows, in the local paper, in community centres etc. As with all other carers, interview thoroughly, ask for and follow up all references.

Housekeeper. If you have previously employed a nanny, plus cleaner, plus done a lot of your own cooking, the idea of a traditional full-time housekeeper may not seen anachronistic when you consider it carefully. Having someone to wash, iron, shop, clean, pick up the children from school and give them tea, *and* have something hot and delicious simmering in the oven for you when you arrive home tired and hungry starts to look increasingly attractive if you can afford it. Set about finding someone from nanny/mother's help agencies, see Chapter 5.

Organised Out-of-School Schemes

The schemes most useful to working parents are the 'kids' clubs', which typically run from 3.30 pm until 6 pm on working days. If they have suitable premises, many will open all day during school holidays, too. Some are run in school buildings, others operate from community or leisure centres, scout huts, village or church halls or purpose-built premises. Standards vary, but a good scheme will collect children from school, offer a snack and a drink, then trained play workers will keep them entertained with a range of activities, quiet and noisy, lively and sedate, until they are collected by parents or another named adult. Fees are usually on a sliding scale, based on ability to pay, but are low compared to other forms of childcare. Some schemes give priority to single parents.

How to find an out-of-school scheme

Under the Children Act, any out-of-school services catering for children under eight must be registered with the local Social Services department. It is a good idea to contact them first, although a variety of departments may be involved in different sorts of out-of-school provision. If you find the local authority unhelpful, try the Kids' Club Network (see page 205 for the address), who keep a national directory of schemes. And keep your ear to the ground—other mothers can often hear of useful projects before they become 'official'. Another source of information will be your local working mothers' group.

What To Do If It All Goes Wrong!

Unfortunately, even schools cannot be relied on to open 100% reliably (there's always the possibility of teachers' strikes, heating breakdowns, classes cancelled), so a wise working mother needs a back-up arrangement of some kind. Building up goodwill and storing up small obligations with friends and neighbours can repay handsomely if they will step into the breach in an emergency. Otherwise try:

Local support groups. Your local branch of the Working Mothers Association or National Childbirth Trust may help in an emergency, but join now and contribute, otherwise your panicking phonecall may meet a rather frosty reception.

Paid agency help. This is best kept for when all else fails or for one-off days, as it can be extremely pricey and rather unsettling for the children if you get a different person each day. However, some domestic/nanny agencies can provide someone at short notice. Some larger agencies have a national network, so if local firms can't help, look through *The Lady* magazine.

Starting Your Own Kids' Club

As previously mentioned there are only 400 out-of-school schemes in the whole of the country, and a third of those are in London, although there are still some boroughs with no provision at all. If you discover there is nothing suitable near you, try getting together with other working parents to set up something yourselves. While the thought of committing yourself to more work raises a groan, you could limit your role to that of initiator—determining the support for such a club among other parents at school, and calling the first meeting, for example, before handing over to someone else with more time to spare. Be warned, however, that such projects can take several years to get going, so you may need to start pre-school if you wish your children to benefit.

Ros Weatherall, who tried to start an after-school club at her daughter's school, advises: 'Treat it as a long term project. Always start *before* you need it yourself. Children won't wait—if you delay they'll be too old by the time it opens!' Ros was thwarted when a local headmaster changed his mind about allowing the club to use school premises, but others took up where Ros left off, and an out-of-school scheme was eventually established in the newly built tenants' hall on a nearby housing estate.

Kids' Club Network estimate that 25,000 out-of-school schemes are needed countrywide to meet demand, but this won't happen without pressure from parents. They can provide expert advice and on-going support to parents who wish to set up their own scheme. Their excellent do-it-yourself advice pack, *Up, Up and Away*, covers all the vital areas, such as finding premises, obtaining funding, legal aspects, health and safety, hiring staff etc. In some areas of the country they have development workers who can give hands-on help when the going gets tough.

'The hardest part is keeping the enthusiasm and interest going,' says Carmen Lindsay, a single mother of two, who helped set up the Camberwell After Schools Project (CASP) in south-east London. 'There are times when you feel like giving up—that's when it really helps to have KCN support.'

CASP was founded by a group of single parents who needed after-school and holiday care for their primary school age children. Carmen first drew up a questionnaire and handed it out at her daughter's school. There was a lot of support, and after approaching several local schools the CASP project were granted the use of school premises. The club was set up first on a voluntary basis, with parents contributing time as supervisors, then in 1986 the scheme successfully applied for a Department of Environment grant and were able to take on paid workers. Finally in 1990 they moved into a purpose-built centre. Now CASP provides 30 places for five–11 year olds, with local children going on to the waiting lists as early as six months old!

Another scheme which started small and has gone from strength to strength is the Bristol Association of Neighbourhood Daycare (BAND). Established ten years ago by three single mothers who joined forces to provide some much-needed daycare facilities, the scheme has grown into an umbrella organisation for after-school and holiday schemes, and receives enquiries from all over the world! BAND provides support and training for emerging kids' clubs; not surprisingly there is now a network of successful clubs across Bristol.

Working mother Kim FitzGerald is sponsorship development manager for BAND, and is also on the committee of her son's after-school club. She admits it takes time and commitment to start up a club, but points out 'the most successful and enduring clubs are those which have been started by parents who really need them'. She is now only required to attend a committee meeting every six weeks; in return she has complete peace of mind about her son, who is collected without fail every afternoon from his school and enjoys a variety of supervised activities with his friends until Kim is able to pick him up.

Coming Home Alone

As children grow up, the dilemma for all parents is the need to protect them without restricting their freedom and personal development. 'Children need care, but they also need the opportunity to grow,' is how Tess Woodcraft, director of the Kids' Club Network, expresses it. While campaigning actively for more out-of-school schemes, she acknowledges the 'tension between children's need for care and supervision and their need for independence and self-determination which becomes increasingly apparent as they grow older'. The issue often comes to a head when they start to ask if they can come home from school by themselves, before you return from work.

Despite a widely held belief to the contrary, there is no minimum legal age at which a child can be left alone. However, the Social Services can bring a prosecution for neglect against parents who regularly leave young children unattended. The commonly held view that you are not supposed to leave a child under 14 alone (which the NSPCC cite as one of the 'top ten' most mistaken beliefs about children) may arise from confusion with the age at which a child can be held legally responsible, which is 16. It is up to you as a parent to decide when your children can be allowed more independence.

The term 'latchkey' child conjures up all sorts of horrid images, fuelled by the media, and will naturally play on the guilt-susceptible working mother. Try not to let it colour your judgement, as guilt can make you over-protective. There have always been sensible older children able to come home alone. Social pressures, newspaper horror stories, nightmare traffic all encourage us to almost over-cosset our kids, when fostering their independence might be a more valuable way to prepare them for adulthood.

Provided children are fully prepared and 'trained' by you to be aware of the hazards, walking home from school or using public transport gives them a sense of freedom and encourages responsible behaviour. You are saved time and hassle and there's one less car on the road.

IS YOUR CHILD READY TO COME HOME ALONE?

This 12-point checklist, taken from an American publication, *The Handbook for Latchkey Children and Their Parents*, by Lynette and Thomas Long may help you decide if your child is ready to cope alone after school on a regular basis.

1. Do you consider your child old enough to assume self-care responsibilities?
2. Do you believe your child is mature enough to care for him- or herself?
3. Has your child indicated that he or she would be willing to try self-care?
4. Is your child able to solve problems?
5. Is your child able to communicate with adults?
6. Is your child able to complete daily tasks?
7. Is your child generally unafraid to be alone?
8. Is your child unafraid to enter the house alone?
9. Can your child unlock and lock the doors to your house unassisted?
10. Is there an adult living or working close by that your child can rely on in an emergency?
11. Do you have adequate household security?
12. Do you consider your neighbourhood safe?

The authors say that if you have had to answer 'No' to any of the above, 'it is strongly recommended that you delay or abandon plans to leave your child in self-care until positive responses can be given for all the questions'.

Preparing Your Children to Cope Alone

If you decide to let your child come home alone, there are various safety aspects to consider.

Home safety

Dr Sara Levene, medical consultant to the Child Accident Prevention Trust (CAPT), says begin safety training as early as possible, explaining why certain household equipment is dangerous rather than just issuing dire warnings about 'hot' or 'sharp'. As children get older, Dr Levene suggests a joint effort towards safety. 'Go round your house together, asking children what possible dangers they can identify. In this way you can discuss things together, the information sinks in without you "lecturing". Make sure children know how to operate household equipment like kettles and microwave ovens and let them practise under supervision—it's sometimes surprising how inept even teenagers can be at first.'

Emergency drill

Work out a procedure in case of a fire (do they know the quickest way out, whom to go to for help?). Have several dummy runs. Stress that they must never try to put out the fire themselves but leave the house immediately. Post up a list of essential numbers by the phone: your work, emergency services, nearest doctor, local police station, numbers of nearby friends and neighbours. Ensure your children know exactly how to dial 999 and how to give their name, address and telephone number in full. Teach them some basic first aid for use in less serious incidents.

Travel safety

Practise the route home with your child, whether walking or using public transport, until you are sure he/she knows exactly what to do. If walking, try to find the safest, not necessarily the quickest route back from school, using crossings and avoiding any unsavoury areas. Investigate bus maps—there may be one which takes a less direct route but drops off in a safer place.

Reiterate all the warnings about talking to strangers and accepting lifts. Make it absolutely clear that women can be just as dangerous as men, and even those who appear to be respectable or claim to be doctors, teachers etc. must not be trusted.

Once at home

Tell them not to open the front door to anyone. Teach them how to answer the phone without revealing you are not there. Suggest a home alone routine, which will give an added sense of security, for example ring mum at work to 'check in', change out of uniform, make snack, start homework. You could also include a few simple supper preparations like 'scrub potatoes'! (See Chapter 9 for ready-prepared, single portion meals which can be simply and safely reheated in a microwave by older children.)

Always be aware of the need to keep lines of communication open—it's vital to make time to talk when you return home from work, even if it's while you all flop in front of the television. It's better to be relaxed about this rather than setting up a formal 'chat' session which is guaranteed to send sensitive teenagers scurrying to their bedrooms. It's often easier to broach problems over simple chores when they feel less pressurised.

Help for the Holidays

Children have about four months' holiday a year from school—if you subtract your entire leave allowance (usually one month) that still leaves one-quarter of the year to cover! The long summer break presents most problems for working mothers, apart from those who are teachers or who are married to teachers. Some employers now offer term-time working or make it possible for women to work from home for part of the time. (See Chapter 11 for more flexible working ideas.)

However, most mums have to muddle through with a variety of help. Relatives, particularly parents and in-laws, are in great demand, often invited for a couple of weeks' 'break' in return for keeping an eye on the kids. If you don't have family as an option, here are some alternatives:

Childminders. Some will take children throughout the summer holidays. If you can find a teacher who uses one during term time and pays a retainer for her place during the holidays, you might be able to 'share' by taking the vacant place during the summer.

Share a nanny with a school teacher—try your child's school first or try advertising locally. If you have previously employed an excellent nanny full time you could, with her agreement, advertise her for a share with a school teacher.

Employing a student/trainee. Ideally, a trainee nursery nurse or similar, on holiday from a local college. They'll be keen to get the experience, and fairly cheap. Student teachers may also be willing, if they live locally. (Find your nearest NNEB course by contacting head office, see page 204 for the address.)

Holiday playschemes. An increasing number of local authorities and voluntary groups are beginning to work in partnership with local employers to provide these schemes. Some employers now offer summer schemes for the benefit of their employees; Boots' head office in Nottingham began a scheme after pressure from its working mothers group. Other schemes are run by voluntary groups, and some are an extension of existing out-of-school clubs, which have suitable premises for day-long occupation. Most schemes operate for the benefit of working parents and open from 8.30–6 pm every day throughout the summer.

Reading Borough Council provide an excellent range of community-based out-of-school care, which includes two holiday 'play clubs'. These are designed to look after children from five–11 years and are open every day during the summer holidays from 8.30 until 6. There is a wide range of activities, arts and crafts, music, indoor and outdoor games. Children are supervised at all times by qualified playworkers, and are registered on arrival. Fees range from 75p to £4.20 a session.

Information about similar schemes can be obtained from your local authority, but you may have to ask which department handles it, possibly leisure and amenities, not necessarily Social Services.

Holiday camps/adventure holidays. Privately run day camps, 'adventure weekends' and residential holidays can offer children a great deal of fun and excitement. However, they tend to be expensive and are obviously only a partial solution to the holiday care problem. PGL Adventure Holidays are one of the longest established companies, running activity holidays all over Britain, which cater for children aged six to teenagers up to 18. They also run a summer day camp for eight–16 year olds at Rickmansworth in Essex. The fully escorted travel service, which PGL and other companies offer for an extra charge, is a great bonus to busy working parents. As a rough guide, PGL prices start from around £250 for a week, weekends from around £80 and day camps £20. For a list and description of approved adventure holiday camps, contact the British Activity Holiday Association (see page 205) who regulate the quality and safety of member companies.

Summer schools. Many boarding schools run activity weeks (often playing host to holiday companies as described above) or run special interest courses themselves during the summer holidays. Residential holidays tend to take the over-sevens, but some schools offer 'day camps' with a range of activities for younger children, some as young as three. Contact the Independent Schools Information Service (see page 206) for their summer school supplement, price £1, or contact your local education department.

CHAPTER 8
Coping Single-handed

'I came to parenthood with very low expectations, believing that babies cried all the time and stopped you doing anything worthwhile. As a single parent I looked for even less joy. I had a wretched picture of the single mother as a walk-on part in *Les Miserables*, a down-trodden hag rearing a new generation of social problems in squalor. It therefore came as a surprise to find that single parenthood has positive advantages.'

Bestselling author Celia Brayfield, writing in *SHE* about the joy and occasional pain daughter Chloe has brought to her life. Celia found that while officially she might be described as a 'social problem', her economic and emotional freedom to choose makes her the envy of many mothers in 'normal' relationships: '"You are lucky, Celia", said my friend Julie as we took her children round to my house for a bath—her husband's £30,000 sports car was in the drive but he didn't think it was worth spending money on a new boiler. "You're so lucky", mutters another friend who loves her job but gets endless nagging from her mother about neglecting the children. "I wish I had your problems", announced Diane, after admitting that her husband travelled so much that she was a corporate widow with two children, two step-children and no social life at all.'

However, single parents *are* greatly disadvantaged by the way society as a whole perceives their situation. The oppressive combination of media headlines ('one-parent families cost the taxpayer millions') and official pronouncements about 'problem' families make it harder to get your life together. In the face of such negative attitudes it is hard to remember the positive aspects of single parenthood. As well as practical advice, this chapter also offers inspiration from single working mothers, who are determined to count their blessings.

'I can be with my child more than two parents who go out to work,' says Celia Brayfield. 'All around me are mothers who genuinely feel more alone than I am, because their partners are stressed-out, emotionally unavailable or escaping the home on pretext of business, sport or community projects—to say nothing of adultery.'

While often beset with financial woes and childcare headaches, there are many single working mothers who find compensation in the exceptionally close relationship they have with their children; women who delight in the freedom from conflicting demands of partner and family. Lou Coaker, who is a tax inspector with the Civil Service, was in a stable relationship when she became pregnant. Her partner, 'who didn't want the commitment', upped and left after three months, and she has supported her son Joe for the last eight years.

'Joe has my undivided attention at home—I don't have to split my affection. He is with adults a lot, which has made him outgoing and socially confident, and he's able to speak well—his command of language is very mature. I really enjoy his company and we do lots of things together, but he has his own activities too—Beaver Club, piano lessons and so on. He is very good about recognising my need to go out too—he never makes a fuss about being left. Sometimes when I'm feeling a bit low I wonder "why do I have to make all the bloody decisions", but then the plus side is that I don't have to compromise about anything!'

Jane Grant, who set up her own PR company after leaving her husband two years ago, stresses the positive aspects of single parenthood too. Her two children are now 11 and nine. 'My husband was shattered when I left and still loves me, but in a way that gave me strength to forge ahead with my career. His job was always "more important" than mine, and he was rather chauvinistic. I now feel I've found myself; it was a liberating process, even though it was a ghastly one. Now I'm maintaining my own way of life, there's no man to answer to, cook for or look after. My relationship with the children has changed; my daughter said to me that I had learnt how to be a daddy, and my husband had learnt how to be a mummy.

'I'm quite romantic, so I don't have my heart set on being alone forever, but at the moment I certainly don't miss having someone to moan to about work in bed at night. My husband would probably have told me it was all due to a problem with my personality. Anyway, it's bliss having the bed all to myself. I can stretch out and watch telly all night if I want!'

Tricia Emptage, a freelance theatre lighting technician, PHD research student and divorced mother of two boys aged seven and 13, says that she 'has never been happier or more fulfilled. When I was married I felt like a doormat. Now I do what I want, so even the dreary jobs are done (or left undone!) through choice. I would rather spend my spare time with my children, having fun. I don't fuss about trivia and I give the boys lots of freedom and independence, as far as is sensible and safe. The children treat me as a respected friend, which fills me with pleasure.' No wonder her elder son's schoolfriends voted Tricia their 'favourite mum'!

Work and the Single Parent

Coping as a single working mother is complicated by extra childcare problems, but the straightforward necessity to earn money can be emotionally liberating, as it was for Celia Brayfield.

'Most of the complicated decisions modern mothers have to make are simplified for me. There is no question about whether or not to work, or what priority my work should take, because I am the only breadwinner. For me, becoming a single parent was a massive incentive to achievement; the need to secure our future and also be with my daughter propelled me from being a contented but ill-paid journalist to bestselling author.'

Many single mothers who answered the questionnaire for this book stressed the value of work in their lives, practically and emotionally. While several earned barely enough to cover full-time childcare and living costs, they strived to keep a career going through their children's pre-school years. Others who found this impossible and were in fact better off on state benefits, said they missed many aspects of work, feeling the lack of social contact most acutely. Once their children started school they felt more able to return to work or training, but found greater difficulty in achieving the sort of salary needed to support themselves and their children.

Lou Coaker, mother of eight-year-old Joe, appreciates the social benefits of work. Having worked for the Civil Service for nearly 20 years, she is well respected and has a wide circle of friends and colleagues. 'Going out and socialising at night is far harder for single parents, but I don't miss it so much because I have adult company all day.'

However, she has had to balance her work and her commitments as a single mother, which has meant her career has not advanced as far as it might. While this situation is far from uncommon among working mothers *with* partners, Lou has turned down a couple of promotions purely because the extra travelling would mean curtailing Joe's out-of-school activities.

'The good thing about working for the Civil Service is the flexibility of hours, which makes it easier for me to ensure Joe's life is as full and interesting as possible. I can take time off when I need it. As I know my job so well I can work on automatic pilot some days and devote more energy and time to Joe. Maybe that means the job isn't stretching me enough right now, but then Joe is more than adequate compensation.'

Returning to Work After a Break

If you are finding difficulty in making the transition from living off benefits to getting back into paid work, the National Council of One Parent Families can be of great help. They have been running Return to Work courses for single parents since 1987, and a £1,000,000 grant from the Department of Employment has enabled the Council to expand this nationwide retraining programme which tackles the special problems lone parents face when trying to get back to work.

Lack of confidence and out-of-date skills are difficulties lone parents can share with many married women returners, but a single mother experiences additional problems of isolation, unaffordable and complicated childcare arrangements which seem to trap her on benefit.

'Lone parents need personal financial advice in order to ensure that the risky transition from low but secure benefit, to the less secure world of work with all its hidden expenses, will indeed make their families better off,' points out Sue Slipman, Director of the NCOPF. 'Our courses have been very successful in helping lone parents to overcome these problems.'

The six-day courses, run throughout the country (but mainly in inner city areas) cover confidence building, job search skills, help with financial planning and information on finding training, education and local employment opportunities, plus lots of advice on practical problems like childcare. Each course will include input from local authority representatives, local employers and trainers who will be able to give very specific local information. Courses are free for single parents, with free childcare, food and help with travelling expenses. While not promising an overnight success, the NCOPF trainers aim for a 'staged progress' back into employment, and have so far proved very successful.

The NCOPF also produces a comprehensive guide *Returning to Work: a guide for lone parents*, which is available from them free to single parents. This information pack can be used independently or as part of the course.

Having a job which provides an identity, respect and adult social contact is vitally important both practically and emotionally to the single mother. Barbara Medway, who has a daughter of ten, found it impossible to arrange full-time childcare when her daughter was small. She tried to get off state benefits by finding a job when Alice was three, but two bad experiences, an indifferent childminder and then a local authority nursery filled with particularly unruly children forced her to give up her attempt to work until Alice started school. She remembers the sense of isolation: 'When Alice was small I used to go and sit in pub gardens at lunch time to listen to the office workers chatting. I just wanted to hear grown-up conversation.'

Barbara spent a year at college, where her lectures fitted in with Alice's school hours, and then found a full-time job as a quality inspector, working flexi-time. She advertised at her daughter's school for someone to pick Alice up and look after her until she gets home.

'To me work is an essential part of surviving as a single mother. Going in to an office on Monday means there is always someone to ask if you had a good weekend; it means I can still conduct "adult" conversations. I feel I am providing my daughter with a role model of a woman earning enough to buy her own car and keep a roof over her head.'

Getting legal and financial help

If you are faced with supporting a child or children by yourself, it's vital to get as much expert advice as possible, as early as you can.

If you are separating from a partner or husband you will need help to sort out many areas of your life which will be changed. The following can give you advice:

• The National Council of One Parent Families produce a very useful pack *Becoming a Lone Parent after Divorce or Separation.* This covers the divorce procedure, custody and access, maintenance, legal aid, benefits and tax, housing, and details of key agencies who can help.

• The Citizens Advice Bureau will be able to advise you and provide you with a list of local solicitors, including those who operate the legal aid system (find your local CAB in the telephone directory).

• A local law centre, if there is one in your area, will be able to give you detailed legal advice. For your nearest law centre, call the Law Centres Federation on 071-387 8570.

If you are pregnant and faced with the prospect of bringing up your child alone, or perhaps considering doing so out of choice, you are likely to need detailed financial advice to work out just how best to manage, what benefits you will be entitled to even though you want to carry on working, and how best to protect you and your child through insurance, pensions plans etc.

• Ask at your local library if you can consult the NCOPF Information Manual. (If your library doesn't have a reference copy it should—insist that someone orders this extremely useful and comprehensive self-help guide, available direct from the NCOPF.) The section on Personal Financial Planning covers building up an emergency fund through saving, pensions, life insurance, choosing a suitable mortgage and making the most of a sudden windfall. It also contains a list of useful addresses.

• Seek expert advice from your local Citizens Advice Bureau.

• Consult a bank or building society, particularly if you have had a long association with them. While most are tied to one particular life insurance company, many have an independent financial advisory service attached.

• Consult an independent financial adviser. Finding someone competent and reliable is not always easy, although tighter regulations have cleared many sharks and crooks from the arena. Personal recommendation is reassuring, but it is best coming from someone in a similar position as yourself, looking for a way to ensure financial security for dependants. The best advisers offer a sympathetic and friendly, rather than high-powered service, so you could ask them for help in making a career change decision, for example, which might jeopardise your pension arrangements. You might also consider consulting a solicitor or accountant. Accountants are a good bet if you need some sound tax advice as well.

Wendy Malpass, marketing manager of the Birmingham Repertory Theatre and mother of Freya, aged seven months, admits her finances were in a 'bit of a mess' when she first became pregnant. She had just been promoted to manager, and was on a reasonable salary for a single woman; she had a mortgage and various credit card debts which had been tolerable for someone with no other responsibilities. When Wendy realised that her partner did not intend to be supportive in any way, she forced herself to get organised.

'I went first to the Citizens Advice Bureau, and literally burst into tears on their doorstep. They were about to close, but took me in, made a cup of tea and helped me sort things out. I was in a real financial mess—I had always been fairly hopeless with money. My practical and patient brother-in-law helped me work out all my ingoings and outgoings; I paid off all the credit cards and took out comprehensive insurance, health, life and redundancy protection. After seeing my bank manager and building society I worked out a 'calendar' of payments, which I found a real comfort. During the pregnancy, which was fairly fraught emotionally, whenever I felt a bit wobbly I'd grab the calendar and go through it— then I felt in control. I don't think I could have got through the pregnancy if I hadn't got my finances sorted out.'

Like most first-time mothers, Wendy had not really considered the expense of childcare until she was faced with paying out herself. 'I was amazed at the problems, which I'm ashamed to say had never really crossed my mind. I worked out that a single mother in Birmingham needs to earn at least £15,000 a year to be able to afford full-time childcare, a mortgage and all the rest. If I hadn't got the more senior job I would have had to stop working when I had Freya—it just wouldn't have been worthwhile financially.'

Finding childcare: formal and informal

See chapters 3–7 for how to go about finding care, but remember, as a single parent you may well get more attention from your Social Services department. Also, your child will have priority for a nursery place, although in local authority nurseries most of the places are reserved for children deemed 'at risk'. Naturally even

the most dedicated staff are going to have less time for your child
when they have to cope with often very disturbed and difficult
children. Although financially, local authority nurseries are the
most accessible form of childcare for single mothers, you may not
feel happy with the set-up.

However, community nurseries, which take children from the
immediate area and have a sliding scale of fees, usually give priority
to single parents. You may find that while the social mix of children
is more balanced, you have to contribute some time to keeping the
project up and running. If you would prefer a childminder, it's
always worth asking if your local authority offers single parents
any help with paying the fees.

If they live nearby, many single parents depend heavily on
their families for childcare. However, Andrea Hopkin's dedicated
mum comes *ten miles* by bus each day to pick up her grandson
Michael from his school! She has Michael for part of the
holidays, and will come to Andrea's house if he is too ill for
school, starting her journey at 6.30 am so that Andrea will be
on time for her job as administrative assistant in a college
information and advice centre.

'She won't accept payment,' sighs Andrea, who admits that her
wonderful mum tackles the ironing and dusting as well. Andrea
also uses a morning childminder, recommended by the headmaster
at Michael's school, which costs £1 a day. The same childminder
has him during the holidays, at a cost of £36 a week. Some days
during the summer holiday Michael also goes to a subsidised local
playscheme, which cuts down the childminding fees.

Chrissie Lynch, PA to the managing director of a London-based
design company, has come to an unusual arrangement with her
parents, which illustrates many of the dilemmas facing single
mothers who want to work. Chrissie's parents moved from London
to Brighton when they retired. They now look after her son Nicholas, three and a half, during the week, and Chrissie joins them at
weekends. Nicholas attends a nursery school each morning, at a
cost of £80 a month, and a childminder each afternoon, which
costs £37.50 a week.

'I am not a single parent out of choice. My son was born in
Greece, but I realised the relationship with his father was not going
to work so we returned to the UK when Nicholas was 15 months
old. My attempts to find work in Brighton were frustrating; local
salaries were too low to be able to consider childcare, housing etc.

The only answer was to work in London where salaries were higher, but where accommodation for both of us was far too expensive.

'If I lived in Brighton, where the maximum salary is £10,000 if you are lucky, I would still not see Nicholas all day during the week, would still have to pay around £300 a month for a small flat, still pay the same in childcare fees and not know anyone else. Alternatively I could put myself at the mercy of the local authority as a "single homeless mother", but that is not my style.

'In London (where my friends are) I earn a good salary, but not enough to be able to afford accommodation for Nicholas and myself plus the higher childcare fees. So we exist in our current situation. It's not ideal, but Nicholas knows where he is, he has a large house and a garden 100 yards from the sea, a great nursery school, a fantastic childminder and his loving grandparents to keep him in line.'

Jenny, 34, is a Bristol midwife who copes single-handed with a family of five, ranging from age 12 down to six. The shift work demanded by her job, including weekends, makes 'normal' childcare arrangements impossible, so she solved her problem by using a live-in student as babysitter.

'I investigated a childminder, but discovered it would take all my wages. Also, it was unfair to expect the children to stay in someone else's house until 10.30 pm and then be back there at 7 am the day when I'm on the late/early shift. Fortunately I live near a university and several colleges and have a 'spare' bedroom (although my eldest daughter would love it!), so I advertised the room rent free to a student in return for occasional childminding. So far the arrangement has worked well—I have had two Chinese students in two years. (They don't seem to have as much of a social life as English students!)'

Organising a support network

For single working mothers, particularly those without any family nearby, a back-up system to formal childcare is not so much desirable as absolutely vital. A network of supportive women friends can help with both babysitting and fighting off the blues. On the practical side, you may not be able to afford full-time childcare and need family, friends or neighbours to plug the gaps. Without a partner to share 'emergency' cover you need someone else who can step in at short notice should childcare arrangements break down, or you are ill.

The organisation Gingerbread (see page 206) runs a network of local groups for single parents and can put you in touch with your nearest group. These operate as mutual support systems, often skill swapping, with members working a form of barter in babysitting, practical help, odd jobs etc. The national organisation can also give individual advice on any welfare problem, or help in setting up a group if one does not exist in your area. In some areas Gingerbread groups run playgroups and after-school schemes for single parents. Gingerbread have also produced a useful guide, *Just Me and the Kids—a manual for lone parents* (published by NCVO Publications at £4.95). Order through bookshops or direct from Plymbridge Distribution, Estover, Plymouth PL6 7PZ. P & p 62p.

If you are pregnant now, and intend to return to work after maternity leave, then start setting up your own support network as soon as you can. Antenatal classes are a good place to develop relationships with women who have a lot in common! If you can find another single working mother to be, it might be the beginning of a long-lasting and supportive friendship. Postnatal exercise classes also offer opportunities to meet other mothers in the same state as yourself.

Unless your employer offers a particularly generous maternity package, it's likely that you will return sooner rather than later to work. This means that you will have to speed up the rather languorous pace at which local mums get to know each other. Depending on the weather, go and push your brand new buggy to the nearest local greenspot and you will soon meet other mums. However, it may take them two nods, four smiles and a long chat over buggies in the park before anyone mentions coming back for coffee 'sometime'. You haven't got time for these elaborate social niceties—swallow that great British reserve and issue firm invitations on the spot. Most new mothers, whatever their situation, are longing for company and to be reassured that a) they are not going totally mad and b) your baby behaves just as bizarrely as theirs does. You can progress from there!

Get to know your neighbours with children—the same principle applies, seize the moment, knock on the door and introduce yourself. It's highly likely a mother at home all day with kids would love a break and a chat, but you won't know until you ask. You may feel the relationship will be pointless if you are returning to work, but if you can count on her support for a daytime emergency, she will value your services as a babysitter.

Pauline Wood, who works as a warden for sheltered housing for the elderly, is separated and has two children of 11 and 13. She's on call for 24 hours a day, five days a week, and has to drop everything if called by a tenant. Her house, part of the accommodation, comes with the job, which sounds ideal, but she's not allowed to leave the site while on duty.

'The children have to be independent—they know where I am but I'm not always available to them. I've had to develop a brass neck to ask people to take them to clubs, gymnastics, Boys Brigade —even their first day at school.'

However, when a crisis struck, Pauline was glad that she had made local contacts, although that included her ex-husband! 'My daughter Vicky developed a mysterious stomach complaint which worsened over a period of weeks until she reached a virtual state of collapse. The doctor asked me to bring her up to the surgery with a view to going to hospital, but a replacement could not be found to cover for me. My relief, who lives on site, was out and uncontactable. Unbelievably, no one else but my ex-husband (who works nearby in a hostel for the mentally handicapped) knew how to work the call system. Permission was eventually granted for him to cover for me, while a neighbour drove Vicky and I to the doctors, waited with me and then drove us to Casualty. (Vicky was eventually diagnosed as having a severe food intolerance, which we now know is caused by dairy produce, citric acid and certain 'E' numbers.)'

On an emotional level, other women, particularly other single mums, may well turn out to be your staunchest allies. Jane Grant, who runs a PR agency from her home in Warwick, advises: 'The most important thing for a single working mother is to maintain a high level of social contact. You must get out with the girls. I've built up a network of surrogate grannies who will babysit. It's so important to be able to talk about things with other women—as you get older you really appreciate that. That doesn't just apply to single mums either—it's very dangerous to hit the menopause with only your children, a husband and no real friends. I've been very lucky. On my 40th birthday I had 40 girlfriends over for breakfast. Were there any men there? No way!'

Fate has dealt Wendy Malpass a very good local support system —six of the women living in her crescent, several of them single, have had babies all around the same time as her! Now where she lives there is a lot of popping in and out of each other's houses and a pleasant air of camaraderie. 'When I was ill with bronchitis I asked my next door neighbour if she would drop Freya at the childminders,' Wendy remembers. 'Instead she offered to look after her herself, and kept an eye on me, too!'

Tricia Emptage, studying anthropology at Hull University, arranges her childcare through a 'mutual support network' of other single mothers. This was put to the test when Tricia had to have emergency surgery: 'The support system took over—house, kids, shopping, all of it. It was wonderfully reassuring!'

Both the pleasures and the anguish of parenthood are experienced more intensely by the single mother. Rising to the challenge of being both sole breadwinner and nurturer means the buck stops with you—but then all the credit is yours too. Take inspiration and strength from your love for your children, and tell yourself you're all doing just fine. As Celia Brayfield says: 'In spite of everything, most of us make out all right. If we did not, the social evils laid at our door would be much more severe. The truth is that every single parent is a hero.'

CHAPTER 9
On the Homefront

To manage (and enjoy) a career, a home and family while remaining sane, healthy and minimally stressed, a working mother needs all the help she can get. The easiest part is acquiring the labour-saving machinery—essentially an automatic washing machine/tumble drier, a freezer and a microwave. Much harder is getting the human help and support, in the form of partners and, age permitting, children. Surveys show that roughly 80% of working women still end up doing most of the housework, cooking, shopping, chauffeuring and general social organising of the family.

You probably never expected to find yourself in this position. What happened to that splendidly fair division of labour that you and your partner upheld in your balmy, co-habiting childfree days? When he cooked the supper while you polished off some notes for the next day's meeting? Men do less once they are married, and what's worse, it seems we let them. A newly-wed who once boasted of her partner's enthusiasm for loo-scrubbing knows the honeymoon is over when she finds herself picking up his dirty socks from the bedroom floor.

Research has shown that while both partners in a supposedly equal modern marriage continue to pursue their careers, tradition triumphs when it comes to domestic labour. It's as though the institution itself imposes a more conventional role on both man and woman. There is less and less sharing, with the women taking on more housework and shopping, and particularly cooking. This is more easily managed for two, but once you add children a woman can find herself stretched to the limit. A victim of her own efficiency, she now finds it hard to make her partner realise what needs to be done.

It's often the thinking and planning—the crucial 'juggling' which is the most tiring part of managing home and work. When asking women how they cope, they often say their partners will only help if told exactly what to do. Men seem to like shopping, for example, once you've given them a clear list of what to buy. And they may do the odd school run, when provided with three days advance warning and written details of the pick-ups! As one *SHE* reader described it: 'My husband and I follow a weekly rota, pinned up in the kitchen, which means that at least he does his share of jobs. But who always organises the rota? I do!'

Many women find that organisation is harder once your children reach school age and the roles of chauffeur and social secretary are added to your job description. On top of the daily routine, you may be required to think creatively about cooking or to dream up ideas for that looming birthday party.

So don't do it! some of you may cry. Well, maybe you and your family *can* thrive very happily on an exclusive diet of convenience foods; you refuse to be drawn into the one-up-mumship of elaborate birthday parties, and you have shamelessly adopted the Quentin Crisp approach to housework—i.e. after four years the dust doesn't get any worse. Good luck to you—you certainly don't need the help provided in this chapter. The rest of us would love to follow your example ... if we were made from sterner stuff.

If It Feels Good, Bake It!

Few could deny that there's far more to cooking than ensuring you and your family don't actually die of starvation. To provide and nurture is a deeply rooted maternal emotion and cooking is an expression of love. That's why it sometimes makes you feel guilty when you defrost perfectly adequate burgers instead of producing a 'wholesome' casserole, and makes you so furious when partners or children reject a meal you have slaved over; it hurts, because it feels as if they are rejecting you.

Underneath the feminist principles of many an assertive, confident, working woman lurks the niggling voice of years of conditioning—or call it tradition. 'Surely a good mother should be cooking "proper food" for her family?' it slyly whispers. Well, compromise. Resolve to demand more help with housework and shopping, but be a little more creative at the cooker, if it will make you happier. Below are some recipes from the batch cook/freeze/reheat school of cookery which makes weekday catering far less of a chore. And if you'd still like to attempt a dinner party or two (remember dinner parties?), read on for inspiration from the *SHE* guide to stress-free entertaining.

These recipes will appeal to working mothers who enjoy cooking but would like to make it as easy as possible for themselves without sacrificing flavour or interest. To put some variety into the week's menus, try these non-fussy dishes with built-in sauces. They can be batch-cooked, frozen easily in single portions and speedily reheated in a microwave without drying out. Also included are some quick assembly dishes which can be ready in under 30 minutes.

This principle can be adapted for many of your family's favourites, and is useful for large stews and casseroles. If you freeze single portions there is no waste, particularly in an active family when the roll-call for supper changes daily. Defrosting is easy and instructions to serve are so simple that older children can cope unaided, and Dad certainly has no cause to grumble when *you're* kept late at work. Another plus point is that washing up is reduced to the absolute minimum.

To fully benefit from this style of cooking you really need the combined talents of freezer and microwave, otherwise you'll have to adapt cooking/reheating times for a conventional oven. (Most of the working mothers who contributed to this section described them as essential.)

It is assumed that most tinies will have been fed earlier by your carer; these are meals that you, and your partner and school age children will enjoy, but some are suitable for younger ones too.

Also included are several recipes for extremely easy quick cakes, which freeze well and can be defrosted in minutes in the microwave. As well as having an instant contribution for the school bring and buy, you have something on standby for an impromptu weekend family tea.

(Note: all recipes serve four adults, unless otherwise stated. Doubling up for batch cooking is straightforward. Reheating times are for defrosted food only.)

Freezer to Table

Saucy Chicken with Almond Rice

Preparation time: 10 minutes
Microwave cooking time: 1 hour
Equipment: large microwave casserole

4 chicken joints, skinned and slashed
Sauce:
200 ml (8 fl oz) natural yogurt
30 ml (2 tbsp) soy sauce
5 ml (1 level tsp) wholegrain mustard
5 ml (1 level tsp) dried tarragon
10 ml (2 level tsp) paprika
15 ml (1 tbsp) tomato purée
2 garlic cloves, crushed
2.5 ml (½ tsp) seasoning mix

In the casserole, mix all the sauce ingredients. Add the chicken joints and smother in sauce. Cover and microwave for 1 hour on LOW. (NB if your microwave has an autosensor function, this dish can be cooked more quickly on the auto setting for chicken portions.)

To freeze: divide between 4 plastic bags, seal and label.
To serve: on-the-table time: 20 minutes
Equipment: microwave casserole, saucepan for rice

Defrost the chicken overnight or in the microwave following the manufacturer's instructions. Decant the defrosted bags into the casserole and microwave on HIGH for 20 minutes (or 5 minutes per joint used). Meanwhile, cook the rice in boiling salted water, drain, fold in a knob of butter, chopped parsley and a handful of sliced almonds. Serve with a green salad, including a sliced apple or pear if wished. Alternatively, serve with potatoes and a green vegetable.

Fish in Mushroom and Anchovy Sauce

Batch preparation time: 10 minutes
Microwave cooking time: 15 minutes
Equipment: large shallow microwave casserole, food processor with slicer attachment

450 g (1 lb) mushrooms, unpeeled, wiped
50 g (2 oz) butter
salt and pepper
675 g (1½ lb) white fish, cut into 4 equal chunks
5 ml (1 tsp) anchovy essence

Slice the mushrooms finely (in a food processor is the easiest). Place in a casserole with the butter and seasoning and microwave on HIGH for 5 minutes. Add the fish and anchovy essence and cook on HIGH for 10 minutes, or according to the microwave automatic setting for fish.

To freeze: divide equally between 4 plastic bags, seal and label.
To serve: on-the-table time: 20 minutes
Equipment: large shallow microwave casserole

Peel off the plastic bags and decant the fish and sauce into the casserole. Microwave on HIGH for 15 minutes, or 5 minutes per portion used. Serve with colourful vegetables.

Lamb Bredie

Preparation time: 5 minutes
Oven cooking time: 1 hour
Equipment: 4 roasting bags, frying pan, baking tray

1 Spanish onion, sliced
oil for frying
1 green pepper, thinly sliced
2 x 400 g (14 oz) canned tomatoes
10 ml (2 tsp) Muscovado sugar
2.5 ml (½ level tsp) ground cinnamon
salt and pepper
4 lamb chump chops

Fry the onion in a little oil, add green pepper and cook until slightly softened. Add tomatoes, sugar, cinnamon and seasoning and heat gently, stirring constantly. Place each chop in a roasting bag and add a portion of sauce and seal. Place in roasting tin (not forgetting to snip off one uppermost corner of each bag) and cook at 180°C (350°F) mark 4 for 1 hour.

To freeze: leave until cool then freeze in bags with the cut corner folded over.
To serve: on-the-table time: 20 minutes
Equipment: large microwave casserole

Peel off the bags and decant lamb and sauce into the casserole. Microwave on HIGH for 5 minutes per chop. Delicious served with jacket potatoes and 'caramel cabbage': coarsely slice 1 small white cabbage and place in saucepan with about 2.5 cm (1 inch) water and a knob of butter. Cover and cook fairly gently until water has evaporated and cabbage just begins to 'catch'. Remove lid, increase heat and stir cabbage vigorously until nicely browned. (The pan will need soaking before washing up!)

All Right on the Night

It's a good idea to keep basics in both freezer and store cupboard; there are nights when pasta, a bottle of ready made sauce and a handful of grated cheese will do nicely, thank you! Here are a couple of tasty dishes which can be requisitioned from the stores.

Fish in Yogurt

(A delicious variation on fish and chips)
On-the-table time: 20 minutes
Equipment: bowl, grill pan, baking tray

4 large plaice fillets (frozen are ideal)
50 g (2 oz) butter
300 ml (½ pint) natural yogurt
30 ml (2 tbsp) mayonnaise
10 ml (2 tsp) horseradish sauce
5 ml (1 tsp) English mustard
salt and pepper
100 g (4 oz) grated cheese

Place fillets skin side up in grill pan and dot with butter. Grill fairly
rapidly for a few minutes while you mix together the yogurt, mayonnaise, horseradish sauce, mustard and seasoning. Turn the fillets over
and pour on sauce. Grill for 3 minutes and then sprinkle over the
grated cheese. Grill until the cheese is golden brown and bubbling.
Serve with oven chips and petit pois.

Cheese and Onion Savoury

Preparation time: 5 minutes
Cooking time: 20 minutes
Equipment: large rectangular baking tin, mixing bowl

225 g (8 oz) strong Cheddar cheese, grated
1 large onion, chopped
1 garlic clove, crushed and chopped
4 eggs, lightly beaten
225 g (8 oz) rolled oats
30 ml (2 tbsp) chopped fresh parsley
10 ml (2 tsp) French mustard
salt and pepper

Mix all ingredients to a porridge-like consistency and pour into a
well-greased rectangular tin. Bake in the oven at 230°C (450°F) mark
8 for 20 minutes. Serve with a large mixed salad.

Crafty Cakes

Working mums who produce homemade cakes can't be all bad, can
they? If you like cooking, there is something peculiarly satisfying (and
guilt-reducing!) about producing your own cakes or biscuits. Non-
essential for nutrition, they can be appreciated purely as affectionate
treats.

Below are a few ideas for oven, microwave and no-bake cakes which can be mixed together when you're in the mood. They can be kept on standby in the freezer and defrosted quickly in the microwave should hungry hordes descend, or the school fete cake stall need an instant contribution.

Oven Bake

The Essential Chocolate Cake

(A nice firm texture—a good base for a birthday cake)
Preparation time: 10 minutes
Cooking time: 30 minutes
Equipment: two 20 cm (8 inch) sandwich tins lined with baking paper, large mixing bowl or electric mixer

175 g (6 oz) self-raising flour
5 ml (1 level tsp) baking powder
100 g (4 oz) caster sugar
175 g (6 oz) soft margarine
3 eggs, size 2
25 g (1 oz) cocoa powder
10 ml (2 level tsp) instant coffee
45 ml (3 tbsp) very hot water
Icing:
100 g (4 oz) icing sugar
25 g (1 oz) cocoa powder
50 g (2 oz) butter
45 ml (3 tbsp) water
50 g (2 oz) granulated sugar

Preheat oven to 180°C (350°F) mark 4. Sift the flour and baking powder into a large bowl and add the sugar, margarine and eggs. Mix the cocoa and coffee to a smooth paste with the hot water and add to the bowl. Fold together until thoroughly blended. If using an electric mixer, start on the lowest speed and mix the ingredients. As they start to blend increase the speed and beat at top speed for one minute. Divide mixture between two tins and bake for 25–30 minutes, until the tops of the cakes are firm. Turn out onto wire trays and leave to cool, then make the icing. Sift the icing sugar and cocoa into a bowl. Put the butter, water and granulated sugar into a small pan and heat gently until the sugar has dissolved. Bring to the boil and immediately pour into the bowl, stirring to a thin cream. Leave to cool (it will thicken), then use half the mixture to sandwich the two cake halves together, then spread remaining icing over the top.

To freeze: open freeze the cake, then put into a freezer bag, seal and label.

Old-fashioned Teabread

Preparation time: overnight plus 5 minutes
Cooking time: Each cake 5 minutes
Equipment: 1 large mixing bowl, 3 lightly oiled 17.5 (7 inch) ring moulds suitable for microwave

300 ml (½ pint) freshly made tea (a teabag in a half-pint mug will do)
450 g (1 lb) dried mixed fruit
25 g (1 oz) chopped nuts (optional)
75 g (3 oz) brown or white sugar
450 g (1 lb) self-raising flour (can be half white and half wholemeal)
5 ml (1 level tsp) baking powder
20 ml (4 level tsp) mixed spice
3 eggs, size 2
milk for mixing

The night before: put the tea, mixed fruit, nuts if using and sugar in a large mixing bowl and leave to soak.
Next day (or even 2 days later!): stir mixture in bowl to ensure sugar is dissolved. Sift together the flour, baking powder and spices. Beat the eggs. Add alternately to the mixture in the bowl, folding in until well mixed. It's important that the mixture is quite sloppy, particularly if using wholemeal flour, so keep adding milk until you get a very soft, dropping consistency. Divide mixture between three ring moulds and microwave each one on HIGH for 5 minutes. Leave to cool, then ease out of the moulds. Eat buttered—very good for school packed lunches.
To freeze: wrap in a freezer bag. This teabread improves with freezing.

Iced Ginger Cake

Preparation time: 10 minutes
Cooking time: 9 minutes
Equipment: large microwave-safe bowl, one 23 cm (9 inch) or two 17.5 cm (7 inch) microwave ring moulds

100 g (4 oz) butter or margarine
75 g (3 oz) black treacle or molasses
50 g (2 oz) dark Muscovado sugar
150 ml (5 fl oz) milk
3 eggs, size 2, beaten
225 g (8 oz) wholemeal flour
5 ml (1 level tsp) baking powder
10 ml (2 level tsp) mixed spice
15 ml (3 tsp) ground ginger

2.5 ml (½ level tsp) bicarbonate of soda
25 g (1 oz) flaked almonds (optional)
Icing and decoration:
175–225 g (6–8 oz) icing sugar
lemon juice, to mix

Put the fat, treacle, sugar and milk into a bowl and microwave on
HIGH for 3 minutes. Cool slightly while you grease the ring mould.
Stir in the beaten eggs, then fold in all the other ingredients. Pour the
mixture into the ring mould and microwave on HIGH for 9 minutes.
(If using 17.5 cm (7 inch) moulds, microwave on HIGH for 4 minutes
each.) Leave in the mould until almost cold, then turn onto a rack.
To make the icing, mix together the icing sugar and lemon juice. Pour
it over the cake and decorate with slices of ginger.

To freeze: wrap in freezer bags.

No-Need-to-Bake Cakes

Chill-Choc Cake

Preparation time: 5 minutes
Equipment: large saucepan, rolling pin, plastic bag (better still, food
processor with chopping blade), 17.5 cm (7 inch) sandwich tin

225 g (8 oz) digestive or plain broken biscuits
50 g (2 oz) soft brown sugar
100 g (4 oz) butter
10 ml (4 tsp) golden syrup
45 ml (3 level tbsp) cocoa powder
50 g (2 oz) raisins
5 ml (1 tsp) vanilla essence

Place biscuits in plastic bag and push rolling pin across surface until
biscuits are coarsely broken (not too fine), or chop in a food processor.
Melt the sugar, butter and syrup gently together in pan, then add
cocoa and raisins. Cook on medium heat until all is well blended.
Remove from heat and stir in vanilla essence. Stir in biscuits until well
coated, then press into the sandwich tin. Chill in the refrigerator.

Variation: Icing can be added if liked—melt 50 g (2 oz) plain chocolate
with a knob of butter and spread over the cake before chilling.

To freeze: wrap in a freezer bag.

Krispie

This is universally liked—I have never met a child, or even a sweet-
toothed adult, who didn't love it. Bagged up in small sandwich bags

and tied with ribbons it makes an ideal quickie contribution for school bazaars etc. Children over five can make this under supervision— allow one toffee for the cook!

Preparation time: 10 minutes

Equipment: large saucepan, deep 17.5 cm (7 inch) roasting tin

100 g (4 oz) creamy toffees
100 g (4 oz) butter
100 g (4 oz) marshmallows
175 g (6 oz) Rice Krispies

Melt together toffees, butter and marshmallows over *very gentle* heat until a gravy like state is achieved. Remove from heat and stir in Rice Krispies 50 g (2 oz) at a time until all the cereal is well coated. Press the mixture evenly into the tin using the palms of your hands or the back of a tablespoon to make a firm 'cake'. Leave to harden—a cool place is better than the refrigerator—and it will be ready to cut into cubes in roughly 1 hour.

To freeze: cut into cubes and put in a freezer bag.

Stress-free Entertaining

What—dinner parties too? No way, you may protest. The thought of all that panic—the cooking, laying the table, putting the children to bed and *then* trying to look glamorous, after a hard day at the office—puts some people off the idea of entertaining all together. But it doesn't have to be this way.

Entertaining really can be hassle-free, if you don't try to dazzle your guests. Forget about fancy dishes from cookery books by famous chefs. While food is undeniably important, remember that what you are doing when you invite people over for a meal is giving them the chance to relax and enjoy the evening together. And that includes you.

After all, the pressures of a career often leave you with little time or energy for dining out. When children come along, energy is even shorter and babysitters can't be found. You talk to your friends on the phone from time to time, but face-to-face contact becomes as rare and luxurious as beluga caviar. That's why dinner parties are important: they provide one of the few occasions when busy people can catch up on the gossip and have a good chat free from the pressures of work and life.

For those pleasures, a little effort is eminently worthwhile. And entertaining is easy if you remember the basic points outlined

below. One point which can't be emphasised too strongly is the
importance of having a plan of action. You can do this on paper
the evening before your party, or even on the bus coming home.
When will you need to preheat the oven? How long will everything
take to cook? Which pots and serving dishes will you need? The
more you can 'visualise' what you'll be doing, the easier it will
be. (Don't forget your partner's contribution—regardless of his
culinary skills there is always something he can do, if only putting
the children to bed!)

Easy Entertaining Tips

- Don't attempt to cram all the work into one day. Last-minute
panic is the enemy of enjoyment.
- Make a plan of action which includes help from your partner
—don't do it all yourself.
- Good meals needn't be hot ones and cold dishes can be prepared
the night before.
- Don't neglect the easy extra touches: crudités and a dip to serve
with drinks, fresh flowers on the table, a proper tablecloth and
napkins, exquisite chocolates with the coffee. They all help.
- Soup is a welcome starter and many, such as vichyssoise and
carrot with fresh mint, can be made in advance, frozen, defrosted
and eaten cold. Just add cream at the last minute.
- Other easy starters include roasted vegetables with a garlic vin-
aigrette, *ceviche* (fresh fish 'cooked' overnight in a marinade of
lime juice, onion, chillies and herbs) and guacamole studded with
a large handful of chopped prawns (add the prawns just before
serving).
- A last-minute starter which takes no work at all and tastes
delicious is avocados stuffed with sour cream, mint and chives
(use really ripe avocados). Avocados also go well with smoked
salmon or halibut, and look good if arranged on pretty little
plates.
- As a main course, braise a piece of beef the evening before and
reheat it or serve it cold with a pungent dipping sauce. A braised
shoulder of lamb or pork should be eaten hot, but can be cooked
in advance and reheated. Poached or roasted free-range chicken
can be served hot with gravy or cold with homemade herb and
anchovy mayonnaise. Baked salmon tastes good straight from the

oven or left overnight. Or serve a simple pasta dish such as Penne all Romana (see below).

● To finish, try a simple fruit salad or another pudding made with fresh fruit. Or skip pudding altogether and serve a cheese board with biscuits, seedless grapes and apples.

The Stress-Free Menu

With all these dishes, much of the work can be done the evening before and the rest will take no time at all. This is the kind of cooking that turns your last-minute scramble into a leisurely stroll. Finally, never forget that the most important ingredient in your dinner party is you. If you enjoy yourself, your guests will too.

Penne all Romana

The vegetables can be cooked the night before. If you can't find ripe beef tomatoes, use red peppers instead. Mozzarella may be substituted for the ricotta.

Preparation time: 25 minutes
Cooking time: 30 minutes

Serves 6

6 beef tomatoes or 6 large red peppers
2 garlic gloves
60 ml (4 tbsp) extra virgin olive oil
2 medium aubergines, weighing about 675 g (1½ lb)
175 g (6 oz) ricotta cheese
4–8 fresh basil leaves
400 g (14 oz) penne rigati
freshly grated Parmesan cheese

If using tomatoes, plunge them into rapidly boiling water for 10 seconds. Peel, seed, and cut into 0.5 cm (¼ inch) dice. If using peppers, grill or roast in a hot oven until the skins are blackened, then peel and deseed. Cut into 0.5 cm (¼ inch) dice. Crush or mince garlic. Heat 15 ml (1 tbsp) of the oil in a large frying pan and add garlic and tomatoes or peppers. Cook rapidly, stirring, for 3 minutes. Remove to a strainer placed over a bowl and set aside. Top and tail aubergines and cut into 0.5 cm (¼ inch) dice. In the same pan, heat remaining oil and cook aubergines for 10–15 minutes, stirring frequently, until just soft. Remove to a bowl. If making the night before, let vegetables cool, cover tightly and refrigerate.

Bring a large pan of salted water to a rapid boil. Chop ricotta into chunks and tear basil into small pieces. Boil penne for 10–12 minutes until *al dente*. Meanwhile, reheat aubergines and tomatoes in a frying pan or microwave them for 3–4 minutes on MEDIUM. When pasta is done, drain well and pour into a large serving bowl. Mix in ricotta, basil and vegetables. Serve immediately with Parmesan passed separately.

Boeuf à la Mode

French cooks use rump for this classic dish, but topside or top rump can be substituted. It has to be started two days in advance, but that leaves you very little to do on the night. If you want to serve it cold, add a pig's trotter to the casserole so the stock will gel.

Preparation time: 20 minutes, plus 24 hours marinating and 24 hours cooling
Cooking time: 2½–3 hours

Serves 6–8

1.5 kg (3¼ lb) piece of boned rolled beef
1 bottle good red wine
4 carrots
1 large onion
2 garlic cloves
1 bay leaf
large handful of fresh herbs, tied in a bundle with string, or a bouquet garni
black pepper
45 ml (3 tbsp) olive oil
225 ml (8 fl oz) beef stock
15 ml (1 tbsp) salt
1 pig's trotter, roughly chopped by the butcher (optional)

Put beef in a large bowl with wine, roughly chopped vegetables and garlic and herbs. Season well with black pepper and marinate overnight. Next evening, preheat oven to 180°C (350°F) mark 4. Remove meat from marinade, dry well, and brown in olive oil on all sides in a large casserole. Add marinade, stock, salt and pig's trotter, if using. Cover and cook for 2½ hours, turning two or three times.

To serve hot: When the meat is cooked, remove from oven and leave to cool. Cover tightly and refrigerate. The next evening, skim off fat from cooking liquid and reheat at 140°C (275°F) mark 1 for 20–30 minutes. Slice thinly and serve with cooking liquid.

To serve cold: Remove cooked meat from casserole and cover with foil. When meat is cool, wrap well in foil and refrigerate. Meanwhile, remove pig's trotter and skim fat from the liquid. Put liquid through a fine sieve, pour into a jug or bowl and refrigerate. Remove meat from the refrigerator 30 minutes before serving and slice thinly. Serve with jellied stock and a pungent sauce, such as salsa verde.

Chicken Brochettes with Watercress Salad

If you don't eat meat, this can also be made with cubes of monkfish.

Preparation time: 5 minutes, plus 24 hours marinating
Cooking time: 15 minutes

Serves 6

350 g (12 oz) boneless chicken pieces
juice of ½ lemon
15 ml (1 tbsp) chopped fresh thyme or 5 ml (1 tsp) dried
30 ml (2 tbsp) extra virgin olive oil
1–2 bunches watercress
salt and freshly ground black pepper

The evening before, skin chicken and trim off any visible fat. Cut meat into 2 cm (¾ inch) cubes (about 30–40 pieces). Combine lemon juice, thyme and 15 ml (1 tbsp) olive oil. Put chicken in a glass or ceramic bowl and pour marinade over. Toss well (this is easiest by hand) and leave it to marinate overnight in the refrigerator. Trim watercress and wash thoroughly, wrap in clean tea towel and leave in vegetable compartment of refrigerator.

Remove the chicken from the refrigerator 30 minutes before eating, and thread on to six small bamboo skewers. Put watercress in bowl and toss with remaining olive oil. Divide it between six plates to make 'nests' for the brochettes, and season each nest lightly with salt and pepper. Preheat grill for 5 minutes and grill brochettes for about 10 minutes, turning two or three times, until just done. Put one brochette on each of the plates and serve immediately.

Syllabub with Kiwi Fruit

This can be made well in advance if you wish, and frozen ready to serve in dishes or cups, covered in cling film. Allow to defrost gently in the refrigerator throughout the day.

Preparation time: 10 minutes, plus 12 hours for infusion

Serves 6

1 lemon
brandy
50 g (2 oz) caster sugar
scant 300 ml (½ pint) sweet white wine or sherry
300 ml (½ pint) double cream
slices of kiwi fruit, to decorate

The evening before, peel lemon thinly, using potato peeler, and place peel in a jug. Squeeze juice and pour over peel, then add enough brandy to make up to 65 ml (2½ fl oz). The next evening, strain the liquid and reserve; discard peel. Add sugar and stir until dissolved; then top up with sweet wine or sherry. Whip cream until just holding its shape (don't let it get too stiff), and gradually fold in the liquid a little at a time. The mixture should stand in soft peaks. Pile into six small serving glasses or cups (demitasse coffee cups are ideal) and chill. Decorate with slices of kiwi fruit and serve with a crisp luxury biscuit such as langues de chat.

Baked Bananas in Skins

There is no simpler pudding in the world, and few that are more delicious.

Cooking time: 25–35 minutes

Serves: 6

6 ripe bananas

Preheat the oven to 180°C (350°F) mark 4. Put bananas, unpeeled, on a large baking tray and bake in centre of oven for 25–35 minutes until a knife goes in easily. You may peel the bananas before serving, but in my experience your guests will enjoy doing the peeling themselves.

Serve with a good quality vanilla ice cream or single cream flavoured with ground cinnamon, or a Cointreau-flavoured whipped cream. If you want to leave out the calories, wedges of lime are a perfect foil for the natural sweetness of bananas.

And Now . . . The Housework!

Ask an experienced (and honest!) working mother how she copes with the never-ending job of housework and she's likely to mention one, or both, of the following: a) lower your standards dramatically b) train your partner. Whether one is a natural result of the other depends on your personal fastidiousness and your partner's competence with the vacuum cleaner, but one thing is for sure— you can't do a full-time job, feed and minister to a family and keep your house spotless, without falling into the 'vicious exhaustion/ guilt circle'.

Once on this joyless merry-go-round, identified by Shirley Conran in *Down With Superwoman* (Sidgwick & Jackson), it is hard to get off. You feel guilty because you work, so you rush around trying to do everything single-handed until you are exhausted; you feel guilty because you're too exhausted to work . . . and so it goes on.

Avoid starting this process in the first place by being resolute in the face of domestic chaos. Just do what you can't avoid. It's not easy; as a professional you are used to things being under your control, to doing a good and thorough job on everything you tackle. But that way madness lies. Accept that your knickers will be unironed, your net curtains less than sparkling and your doorstep distinctly unscrubbed. Or do what matters to you most—recognise your limitations and cut out all the things you really hate doing. Your reward will be far more energy and time to enjoy your children, your partner and the work you get paid to do.

Alternatively, get a cleaner. This is not a financial, or desirable possibility for everyone, but many working mothers employ someone just to do the regular boring but necessary stuff, vacuuming, dusting, bathrooms and loos, etc. Even just a couple of hours a week helps keep things under control, or perhaps just to tackle the ironing. If the principle bothers you—see it as 'buying back time for yourself'. This working mother was glad she overcame her scruples: 'It's hard to describe the bliss of coming home after Christine has been in to clean. Every surface shining, the sink clear, the bathroom really fresh. I can feel myself calming down after a hard day, I stop nagging at the children and for some strange reason, I feel like a proper mother.'

A good idea is to have a cleaner on Fridays, which means you enjoy maximum benefit over the weekend. Less distracted by chores, you'll feel more like enjoying yourself with the family.

The working mothers who contributed to this book by filling in questionnaires demonstrated varying degrees of frustration with their partners when answering the sections on housework, but one thing was clear—if you don't ask, you don't get. 'Train your husband well!' advised one. Here is a selection of their sanity-saving tips:

• Never go up or down stairs empty-handed.
• Always take off your work clothes the second you arrive home, preferably before you pick up any child!
• Shop mail order, and in bulk.
• Organise a simple jobs rota with your partner, to stop resentment building up.

- If you can afford it—a dishwasher is wonderful. It keeps the kitchen tidier, too.
- Clean the bathroom while your children are in the bath.
- Set washing machine overnight. Use Economy 7 and you'll save money as well as time.
- Iron little and often—a mountain is so daunting you'll put it off for ever.
- Only iron essentials.
- Wipe the cooker after every use and you'll never have to clean it.
- We went without a holiday to buy a dishwasher and tumbledrier. Was it worth it? Absolutely!
- Get everything ready the night before for everyone in the house, not just the children.
- Make jobs a family responsibility—either allocate everyone a regular job (NB they must like doing it, otherwise this fails), or allocate a certain period of time when everyone has a blitz once a week. Set an alarm clock and when it goes off—that's it. Everyone working together for half an hour can work miracles.
- Shop without children.
- Resist the temptation to bundle dry clothes into a heap when you're in a rush—this makes twice as much work. Give yourself time to shake out clothes from the tumbledrier or line and fold carefully, and most ironing can be avoided.
- If you and your partner can get a reasonable midday meal at work and the children are being fed by your carer, then agree to eat a lunch out regularly. This saves so much work on weekday evenings.
- Write lists for everything.
- Try to do one spring cleaning type job a week, then no need for mammoth effort.
- Don't bother dusting—run a damp cloth over worst offending surfaces.
- Housework only gets done the evening before visitors are expected—much to the disgust of my chauvinist husband!
- Use bribery—pocket money for jobs.
- If there is considerable support among colleagues, ask for a small fridge/freezer at work. Those who have no alternative to lunchtime shopping can at least buy for several meals in one go.
- Encourage your children to be as independent as possible—they can dress themselves from two and a half.

One working mother summed it all up by applying the principles of her educational management course to running her home: 1) Make lists 2) Prioritise 3) 'Manage' time to reduce stress 4) Delegate whenever possible 5) Cut out all inessential tasks.

No-panic Parties

Last but by no means least, some ideas on the annual angst of birthday parties. Naturally you want your child to have fun, to feel special, to be celebrated. Naturally you feel slightly piqued by his or her breathless praise of the fab party Damien's mum threw last week. And naturally, you know that as usual you have neither the time nor energy to match it. So don't try. There are plenty of ways to have a good time without staying up until midnight crocheting party bags or stencilling place cards. The comments below prove many other working mothers feel the same way:

- Hire a magician—it keeps the kids entranced and it gives you time to slip off to the kitchen for a quick gin!
- Dads are by far the best at organising parties. Leave them to it —they love taking all the credit.
- Buy things when you see them, presents, party props, whatever time of year.
- If your child's at nursery, make it fun for everyone. Take a cake and little presents for games, and let the staff do the rest.
- Bouncy castles are worth every penny. We hire one every year now.
- Investigate your local sports hall or leisure centre. Many now do organised birthday activities, complete with tea at the end. Great for energetic youngsters and no mess for you.
- I buy individual cakes from a local baker and give each child his or her own little picnic in a named box. This cuts down on waste and is especially useful for small boys as it eliminates the mad scramble to grab handfuls of food!
- Small numbers are essential.
- A memorable party was my son's ninth, when we hired the local football club, organised games and tea.
- Video parties are a real cop out!
- Take your child and a few like-minded pals to a major sporting event on the nearest weekend.
- We took our nine year old and his two best friends to an Indian

restaurant, which we all thoroughly enjoyed. (Far more than the previous year, when we had a large party taking one day to prepare and the next to recover!)

● Our two children have birthdays close together, so every four years we have a major splash. (I still invite other mums to help.)

● Swimming parties (you need good adult supervision) are good fun, followed by burger and chips. In winter you can't beat a trip to the panto.

● Whatever you do, don't be drawn into competing for the most elaborate take-home goody bag.

● Buy disposable everything.

● Older children enjoy a trip to a pizza or burger restaurant far more than a party—and now, so do I!

● For my daughter's second birthday I decorated a wooden picnic bench in the park with paper streamers. I took along a picnic tea and a cassette tape with nursery songs and they all played musical statues. Meanwhile, the adults lay in the sun and got drunk.

If you do go for the traditional party at home, rope in as many helpers as you can and strictly limit the number of children. Make a list of all the food you intend to serve—in a rush it's easy to leave items lurking in their plastic bags for weeks afterwards. Entertainers can be a great success—best for the over-fives—but you'll need to have games too, so don't forget to make another list. Have contingency plans in case of disaster; try to avoid this by confirming the booking and providing clear instructions, perhaps even a map, of how to get to your house.

The following are some alternatives for the cake-and-candles weary:

● For junior schoolers, try a 'high tea' party slightly later in the day. Food can be simple, something rapidly warmed up like casserole, jacket potatoes, burgers and oven chips etc. Ice cream with an easy hot fudge sauce (made from melted chocolate bars) to follow.

● Picnics save on mess but need plenty of helpers, particularly if you're all walking to a local park. Specify old clothes on your invitation. Have contingency plans for bad weather.

● 'Dinner Parties' for eight-year-old-plus girls are ideal for a winter evening. The darkness makes them feel very sophisticated. It's easy to make the table look pretty with flowers and candlelight has a magical effect. Ask guests to dress up, serve normal supper food but a bit tarted up, moussaka, lasagne, gammon and pineapple.

Serve cake as pudding, or ice cream and fudge sauce in sundae glasses.

● For sporting eight–14 year olds try match parties—either hire a local playing field or use the park. Depending on preference, organise cricket, football, rounders, book a couple of tennis courts and hold a mini-tournament, followed by a slap-up tea at your local burger bar.

● For those going through a horsey phase, indulge them and take off to a proper event at the weekend (check in an appropriate publication several months in advance). Take several pals, a good picnic, waterproofs and a rug (don't forget binoculars).

● Roller and ice skating rinks can be the destination for a 'mystery' trip (make sure guests bring suitable old/warm clothes).

● Consider air shows, science museums, safari or theme parks as suitable venues.

Have fun!

CHAPTER 10

'Me Time': Go On—You Deserve It!

While a working mother can develop an admirable battery of skills, making time for herself is not something she tends to be good at. Demands on her time and energy come from all sides, it's true, but part of the problem is her inability to yell 'Stop!' even for the sake of her own sanity.

As nervous fliers fear that if they stop concentrating for one moment the plane will crash, so many a working mother will not relax her domestic vigilance. Her day job may be more or less bound by office hours, but she often finds it much harder to set a limit for house and childcare chores, with the result that there is no time left for herself.

'It's endemic to women's experience—the idea that the world will collapse if a certain thing is not done,' says Susie Orbach, founder of the Women's Therapy Centre in London. 'Deprivation of any time for herself can lead to serious stress, and family life suffers when a woman is not being nourished. Every woman has experienced this problem; that's what's so horrifying. They feel selfish, greedy and guilty if they take some time out for themselves.'

Statistics show that women suffer twice as much from depression and anxiety as men. Could a contributory factor be that women's minds have to be in too many places at once—childcare, career, husband, what's for dinner?

'Me time'—a space to recharge batteries, pursue other interests or just to enjoy the peace and solitude of a blissful hot bath—is not a frivolous concept. Devoting time purely to yourself not only helps relax and refresh the mind and body, but also reaffirms a sense of self. It's easy to lose sight of your identity when you seem to exist for others, however much you love them.

SHE reader Elizabeth Gallagher, a social worker from Cleveland, summed this up when completing her questionnaire. She has brought up six children, and recognises the mutual benefits of getting the family to honour 'Me Time': 'I feel strongly that in order to be a good mum (i.e. one who is bringing up her children to respect others and to go out in the world able to cope) you have to be a little bit "selfish". If the children see that you have needs and wants and are prepared to attend to them without guilt, they too will respond to you in a like manner. If you give your all to the children they are liable to see you as a servant or slave—someone without needs.'

Experts say that for the sake of our relationships as well as our physical and mental health we should all make a certain amount of 'me time' sacrosanct. Hopefully, some of the time-saving practical ideas in the last chapter will open up a little more space in your routine, but you won't benefit if you don't allow yourself to fully use and enjoy any spare time you make for yourself.

'Women must give themselves permission to take time out,' insists Susie Orbach. 'The answer is to try to act like an entitled person even if it's only giving yourself two hours a week—hours that are inviolate. Try experimenting with this concept for a month. It may be so unfamiliar you may not know what to do initially, but eventually you should be able to discover things which bring pleasure.'

Several years ago, Gracie, a divorced mother of eight-year-old twin girls, decided to give herself permission to be away from her daughters. 'I have what I call "mummy time",' she explains. 'Once a week, the twins spend the night at my neighbour's house and I use the time to relax completely. Even if there's a pile of ironing staring at me, I won't do it. I usually spend most of the night reading in the bath. It's blissful, and I've discovered that I'm more able to deal with things without being bad tempered. We make a joke out of "mummy time" and the twins are good humoured about it.'

In theory, having a husband or partner around to take the children off your hands should make achieving 'me time' easier. In practice, men often fail to recognise that their partners are being stretched to the limit until bottled-up resentment hits them full force. Men tend to be much better at simply switching off in the face of pressure; it's not that he refuses to help you tackle that huge pile of ironing, it's just that he has gone off duty for the day and can't understand why you don't do the same. It takes a sensitive man to realise that scheduling personal time can be quite a difficult thing for a mother to accomplish, and that his support is crucial.

One way of making sure that time out is honoured is to involve him. Fixing a regular 'date', such as a weekly trip to the cinema, means at least you are not on call for a couple of hours. You could then develop this theme so that you cover for each other one evening a week to allow for solitary pursuits. Spending less structured, intimate time with your partner is important too, and a good way to unwind, but more of that later. First things first— and that means *you* for a change.

Meditation

It may be that solitude and silence are what you miss most. If you devote most of your time to children's needs, endless tasks and social outings, a little time to refocus your mind could be just what you need. Meditation can be extremely therapeutic and it has the advantage of simplicity; all you need is time, space and perhaps a tape to aid concentration.

Meditation can be used on several levels to help an over-stressed working mother, as teacher Kulamitra, a member of the Western Buddhist Order, explains: 'On the simplest level, people meditate because they lead busy lives, are generally quite agitated and find it difficult to calm down,' says Kulamitra. 'On another level, people want to understand themselves better. Meditation is a regular period of time when you're taking your mind away from everyday concerns and allowing it to stretch. Part of that is to look at yourself instead of what's going on around you.'

A Retreat

Another way of securing complete 'me time' is to remove yourself physically from home and work, possibly for a weekend for a complete break. The benefits of a health farm are well documented, but have you ever considered a retreat?

Time for Yourself is an interesting workshop venture run for women by social workers Eileen Peck and Anna Taylor. They offer weekend retreats in the country and the chance for women to examine their lives. 'People spend a lot of time looking after their physical health and not very much time looking after their mental health,' says Eileen. 'We liken our courses to a mental health farm, where you tone yourself up mentally.' Time for Yourself combines relaxation and meditation with discussion, self-assertion and life-planning exercises.

'Our courses encourage women to look at their own internal world and how they operate and how to take control of their lives,' says Eileen. Ironically, she admits that often the women who would most benefit from a weekend retreat are exactly the women who find it most difficult to take time for themselves.

SHE Readers' Suggestions

The working mothers who filled in questionnaires for this book were not 100% successful in achieving 'me time'. While they all appreciated the need, some said that they regarded their jobs as 'me time', because it was time indirectly devoted to themselves and their personal fulfilment. Others could manage no more than half an hour in the bath—but they locked the door and made the most of that!

But it takes determination, particularly if your partner is not particularly supportive. One working mother was motivated by frustration: 'I started putting one evening a week aside for myself when I realised that I was working myself into the ground and my husband was quite content to sit back and let me.'

From other accounts, it seems that the best way of ensuring time for yourself is to make it regular: a certain number of hours each week become known as 'yours'. Attending a class or club seems to command more respect and guarantees babysitting time from partners. Some suggestions from SHE readers:

● We regularly split the weekend into segments—for me, my husband and for 'family time'. I use my segment for a dance class.

● Use a couple of lunchtimes for exercise with colleagues rather than shopping.

● Keep to the same 'me time' every week and you will achieve the same respect as other family members expect for their regular activities.

● Use a self-hypnosis tape to wind down—this is now my saviour.

● Take a full hour's lunch whenever possible and do something you enjoy, go to an art gallery or browse in expensive clothes shops, the sort you could *never* take young children into!

- Exercise—my yoga and aerobics, followed by the pub, are essential to my survival.
- Take the dog for a long, long walk.
- Meditate twice a day.
- Get out of the house—'me time' at home is never successful as I always see something which needs doing.
- Studying, something like an Open University class for example, usually means you are left in peace—children respect that.
- I love to go to the gym—pumping iron and a sauna afterwards is the best way to relax.
- I go to church!
- Take up a musical instrument.
- I take one whole day off work every three months and do absolutely nothing but laze about, play records, read, pluck my eyebrows etc. And once a year I take a week off alone, and although I use some of this for a blitz on the house, I mainly visit friends and relatives I rarely see.

Keeping in Shape

Devoting a little time to keeping yourself in shape will pay great dividends, giving you more energy and vitality to cope with a busy lifestyle. Regular exercise is a great stress beater as well as morale booster, but often busy mums can't spend hours at exercise classes, so *SHE*'s Health & Beauty Editor Louise Pearce has devised this quick and easy daily routine which will tone up your body and increase suppleness in just 12 minutes a day. That way, more sporadic bursts of exercise will not be such a shock to the system! For best all-round fitness this routine should be combined with an aerobic type exercise (swimming, jogging or even taking the dog for a brisk walk) three times a week for 20–30 minutes.

- If you do not exercise regularly, start this routine slowly and gradually build up the repetitions.
- Breathe freely throughout, and if a movement hurts, do not repeat it.
- If you have a history of heart, joint or muscle trouble, always check with your doctor before exercising.

Warm-up routine

Always start your exercise regime with a few gentle movements to get the blood circulating, loosen joints and warm up muscles.
1. With right foot leading, step out to the side and bring your left foot in. Then step out to the side and bring your right foot in. Repeat 8 times.
2. March on the spot for 16 counts.
Repeat 1 and 2 again.
3. Stand with your feet apart, slightly turned out. Slowly bend your knees over your toes. Repeat 8 times.
4. Circle your shoulders backwards 8 times. Circle your right arm backwards once, then your left arm. Repeat 8 times alternating arm circles (8 repeats each arm).
5. Keeping your tummy pulled in, place hands on hips and circle hips to the right, backwards, to the left and forwards. Repeat once. Rotate hips the opposite way twice.
   End the warm-up routine with the following simple stretches. Try to relax and breathe normally as you do them. Do not hold your breath. The more relaxed you feel, the further you will be able to stretch.
Calf stretch. With your feet hips-width apart, step forward with your right foot leading, keeping left heel on the ground. Shift weight forward by bending front knee. Hold for 6–10 seconds. Change legs and repeat.
Front of thigh stretch. Holding on to a chair for support, lift your right heel towards your buttocks and clasp hold of your foot or ankle with your left hand. Hold for 6–10 seconds. Change legs and repeat.

Exercises

Pelvic tilt. Lie on your back and bend your knees, keeping feet flat on the floor and arms by your sides. Flatten base of spine into floor, tightening tummy muscles as you do so. Hold for a few seconds, then relax. Repeat 8 times.
Tummy. Lie as before, but this time place chin on chest and slide hands along thighs towards knees so head and shoulders lift off floor. Hold for a few seconds then lower head and shoulders. Keep tummy pulled in. Relax. Repeat 8 times.
Outer thigh. Lie on side, with underneath leg slightly bent to keep

weight forward. Allow lower arm to support head and place upper hand on floor in front of chest (with arm bent). Keeping upper leg straight, raise and lower it smoothly in scissor movement. Make sure upper hip remains forward and doesn't rock back as you lift. Repeat 8 times.

Inner thigh. Still lying on same side, release outer thigh muscle by bending upper leg and resting it down in front of lower leg. Work inner thigh by straightening bottom leg and lifting it slightly from the floor and lowering. Repeat 8 times, then change sides and repeat outer and inner thigh exercises.

Buttocks. Roll over onto your front, and rest forehead on hands. With buttock muscles tightened and both hips in contact with floor, slightly lift the right leg behind you and release. Repeat 8 times, then change legs and repeat.

Chest and backs of arms. Kneel on all fours with hips straight above knees and hands a little wider than shoulder width apart. Keeping tummy pulled in and back straight, bend elbows and lower nose towards floor. Straighten elbows again. Breathe out as you straighten your arms. Repeat 8 times.

It is important to try and relax while doing the following stretches—don't grit your teeth! Hold each stretch for about 8–10 seconds unless otherwise stated, then *slowly* release.

Hamstring stretch. Lie on your back with right leg bent and foot flat on floor. Bend left knee towards chest and support by clasping hands behind thigh. Then slowly straighten leg upwards until you feel stretch at back of thigh. Change legs. Repeat.

Back rotation. Lie on back with knees bent, feet flat on floor, hips-width apart, arms straight out at right angles to body. With tummy tucked in and back flat on floor, take both knees to right side on to floor. Hold for 3 seconds. Return knees to start position. Repeat to left.

Chest stretch. Stand with feet slightly wider than hips-width apart, your knees slightly bent, tummy pulled in, pelvis slightly tilted forward, back straight and shoulders relaxed. Link hands behind back. Squeeze shoulders and elbows together. To increase stretch, lift arms away from body.

Backs of arms. Stand as for chest stretch. Stretch right arm over head. Bend elbow and lower palm of hand between shoulder blades. Bring left arm across your chest; place hand against right elbow or upper arm. Gradually ease arm back until you feel a stretch. Change arms and repeat.

Beauty: No Time to Lose

An unexpected peaceful hour has come your way but you've nothing to hand for pampering purposes? Raid the kitchen instead and try the following ideas.

• A near-ripe banana makes a cheap but very effective moisturising face pack. After peeling, pulp the fruit and mix with natural yogurt. Apply to your face avoiding eyes (and mouth!) and leave for 15–20 minutes. Wipe with soft tissue and rinse.

• Cucumber is renowned for its refreshing and soothing qualities when used on tired eyes, but did you know it also makes a great astringent for oily skins, helping to tighten pores and reduce shine? Place slices on your nose, forehead and chin—the T zone—or anywhere else prone to oiliness.

• Make your teeth extra white and gleaming by rubbing them with fresh strawberries. Do this two or three times a month and it will help remove tartar.

• Whiten discoloured nails with lemon juice followed by a scrub with white wine vinegar.

• If you suffer from soft, splitting nails, try soaking them for 5 minutes in warm olive oil and then apply a coat of nail hardener. Repeat daily or as often as possible.

• For a monthly hair tonic, beat an egg with a cup of milk and mix it with the juice of half a lemon. Add a tablespoon each of wheatgerm and olive oil and massage the mixture into hair and scalp. Cover with a warm towel and leave on for an hour before rinsing with warm water.

What About 'We Time'?

It's important that you and your partner make time to be together too: time that isn't spent discussing domestic problems or, tempting though it is after a hectic day, frittered away in front of the television. When you live together you take it for granted that you'll have time together, so you no longer plan it. It gets downgraded from an event in itself to something you do between events. This

TEN WAYS TO FEEL AND LOOK FULL OF ENERGY!

- Take a tip from athletes and eat a couple of oranges—a great source of instant energy—when you need a boost.
- Regular exercise will increase your vitality, but if you find it hard to keep the commitment, work out with a friend.
- Try to drink six–eight glasses of mineral water a day to replace the 1.2 litres (2 pints) your body uses every 24 hours to cleanse and cool the system.
- Go easy on alcoholic drinks. Not only are they high in calories but they also stimulate your appetite.
- Feeling tired? Don't let it show—a yellow-toned cover stick will disguise grey shadows under the eyes better than a flesh-pink colour.
- Red lipstick is a great way to add colour to your face—if it's the right shade. Opt for red-oranges if blue-reds leave you looking cold.
- Always apply blusher to your face. Not only will it add warmth and a healthy glow, it will help add some definition to vanishing facial contours, too.
- Keep your hair in shape—it's a real morale booster. Leading trichologist Philip Kingsley says, 'Hair instantly expresses a woman's sexuality—it's the second most sexy thing men notice.' (The first can be left to your imagination!)
- If you're a bit down in the mouth, try a shorter hair cut. It can work wonders to lift your looks.
- Invest in regular beauty treatments. Facials, massage and even manicures can help you to relax after a stressful day. If you can't get to a salon, find a freelance beauty therapist to come to your home.

low-key approach can be relaxing and cosy, but how often does it slip over into boring? And worse, is meaningful communication between you grinding to a halt?

As a mother, you need 'me time'. As a woman in a loving, supportive partnership you also need 'we time'. Every relationship, particularly if under pressure from work and children, needs the occasional boost—call it romance, glamour, or what you will, but make sure your time together is precious.

There's no point going to your favourite restaurant and spending all evening arguing over whose turn it is to pick the kids up from ballet. When you make special time to be with each other, try to make it just that. When you first fell in love, domestic problems were not the first topic of conversation—you talked about your-selves, your hopes, fears, family. Even though it's impossible to recreate those early days you can—just for a few hours—recreate that atmosphere of intimacy, the feeling of sharing yourself.

How you do this depends on your interests. You might both dress up and treat yourselves to a meal—or you might dress down and go for a long country walk. Cooking a meal together can be relaxing, or take it in turns to cook for each other. Even listening to music when the kids have gone to bed can give you space that the TV can't. If you can pack the kids off to their grandparents and spend time at an art gallery or museum, that's even better.

However, before you organise any joint relaxation, remember that one person's wind down can be the other's Chinese torture. When a woman has spent the latter part of the day supervising bathtime and reading bedtime stories while her partner has stayed late for a crucial office pow wow, it is highly unlikely that they will want to relax in the same way that evening. She may yearn to go to a glitzy restaurant or to discuss post-modernist architecture. He probably wants to relax in front of the television.

If you've spent eight hours preoccupied with different things, it may be wise to take a break alone before meeting up for the evening. This will give each of you a chance to clear your heads of the day's trivia. Then, when you do meet, you'll be on, or at least nearer, each other's wavelength.

CHAPTER 11

How to Make your Work Family Friendly

Increasing numbers of working mothers are discovering that new working patterns—flexi-hours, job sharing, term-time working, part time, working from home—allow them to better balance work and family. And more companies recognise that flexibility is a small price to pay to hold on to skill, experience and commitment. Previously the public sector—in particular local authorities—have proved more willing to grasp the nettle of change but now private companies are beginning to offer flexible working arrangements to accommodate the needs of working mothers, even at senior levels.

However, opportunities are not offered on a plate—and you may find if you don't ask, you don't get. Re-negotiating your working week sounds a daunting prospect, but canny employers realise it's better to have a valued employee back on her own terms than not at all. The secret lies in presenting your employer with a well-thought-out proposal, and in being ready to counter objections convincingly.

This chapter offers some useful negotiating tips when tackling your boss, and presents the pros and cons of the various flexible working options available, including some suggestions on retraining for a new, totally part-time career. Working mothers who have broken out of the nine-to-five straitjacket share their experiences, which will help you get a clearer idea of the different ways you can adapt your work pattern.

Remember, though, that while you may feel flexible working suits your schedule, it may not suit your personality. If you're not sure you could cope with handing over responsibility to your job share partner, or that you could adapt to a more fluid power structure, then try the following flexibility assessment, which was specially devised for *SHE* by Cary L Cooper, Professor of Organisational Psychology at University of Manchester Institute of Science and Technology, and Dr Rachel Cooper, senior lecturer in design management at Staffordshire Polytechnic.

Could You Cope With Flexi-Work?

1. Your boss tells you to take on an important job which you feel is outside your area of responsibility and expertise. Do you:
a) Try to get someone else to do it instead?
b) Do it, but reluctantly?
c) Explain to your boss why you feel it should be given to someone else?

2. Work is hectic and you've scheduled your day tightly. Then an old friend you haven't seen for ages turns up unexpectedly. What do you do?
a) Adjust your schedule to accommodate her.
b) Try to put her off until later in the week.
c) Fit her in for a short time only, while still maintaining your schedule.
d) Put her off regretfully and ask her to contact you in advance next time.

3. You are working with colleagues on a job which is completed when you are off work. Your boss takes your colleagues out to lunch to thank them. How do you feel?
a) Left out and upset about it, but blame yourself.
b) Angry at your boss for not acknowledging your contribution to the job.
c) Bothered, but you understand the circumstances.
d) Make a note to remind your boss of your involvement next time you see her.

4. Your partner volunteers to look after the children for a day to give you a chance to go to an art exhibition. What do you do?
a) Accept happily, but worry once you've left as to whether he is coping.
b) Accept very reluctantly and worry all the time you are away about whether he is coping without you.
c) Accept with some reluctance and leave him detailed instructions how to cope.
d) Accept eagerly and go without giving it a second thought.

5. You start a new part-time job. After several months, a colleague who does the same job but works full time is promoted. How do you feel?
a) Bothered, but you accept it with little resentment given your current family situation.
b) Angry with your boss for not recognising your achievements in the company.
c) Upset because you're not working full time.

6. Because you are a busy woman, you employ a cleaner to help with the housework. You return home to find the house has not been cleaned to your satisfaction. What do you do about it?
a) Nothing, but hope the cleaner gets it right next time.
b) Clean the house again thoroughly yourself.
c) Tell the cleaner you're not happy with the job and discuss where it needs to be improved.

7. On one of your days off, something goes wrong at work. A colleague tried to put the blame on you, though it wasn't your fault. How do you react?
a) Defend yourself.
b) Argue it out assertively with your colleague.
c) Just ignore it.

8. You are a very active member of the PTA executive committee at your local school. They want to produce a book of all the children's poems, but on what terms do you get involved?
a) If you can do as little or as much as your time allows.
b) Only if it's on a shared basis.
c) If you can see it through from beginning to end.

9. You return home from work slightly late and your partner is angry that his dinner is not on the table. How do you react?
a) Let him know you feel domestic chores, such as cooking, should be shared.
b) Apologise and rush to get on with preparing the meal.
c) Tell him to make it himself.

10. You work part time, and an important meeting is planned for a day you're not in the office. What do you do?
a) Go, even if it is being held on your day off.
b) Ask your boss or colleagues to attempt to hold important meetings on the days when you're in the office.
c) You wouldn't care.

11. A part-time male colleague is able to commit more of his own time to the job than you are. How do you feel?
a) Totally indifferent.
b) Confident in your ability that, even working the hours you do, you can achieve success in your career.
c) Threatened by him in terms of your career.

How to work out your flexibility score

	a	b	c	d
1	1	0	2	
2	2	0	1	0
3	0	0	1	2
4	1	0	1	2
5	2	1	0	
6	1	0	2	
7	0	1	2	
8	2	1	0	
9	2	0	1	
10	0	2	1	
11	1	2	0	

Now total all your scores for each of the questions. The maximum score you can obtain is 22 and the lowest is 0.

17–22
Your attitude towards work is extremely flexible, making you suitable for job sharing, part-time working and any positions involving quite flexible working patterns. In effect, you are assertive without being too aggressive, adaptable rather than rigid, not controlled by guilt, an organised time manager and reasonably confident of your skills and abilities without being a perfectionist.

10–16
You are moderately flexible in your attitudes and behaviour, but could probably concentrate on learning to be more assertive, to delegate without worrying and not to let your guilt get the better of you when you're working. You should also try to accept that you will have to make quite a few important compromises in order to accommodate your family and work.

Below 10
You could have real difficulty in coping with the demands of part-time working, job sharing or other types of flexible arrangements, to the extent that you may find yourself working longer hours than you would like (or have been contracted to) and feeling upset because your career isn't progressing at the rate you'd like it to. You may not be assertive or even adaptable enough to manage the demands of work and family, and could find yourself having problems coping with the lack of rewards or acknowledgement of your contributions.

How to Win the Contract You Want

- If you are a valued employee you will be negotiating from a position of strength. Your boss should not need much persuading about how valuable your skills are, but be ready to draw attention to them if necessary.
- Your employers' concern will be how it will benefit them, so prepare a well-considered argument. See it from their point of view, rather than simply explaining how it will make your life easier!
- Use threats as a last resort. If you are prepared to resign if your demands are not met you could say so, but gauge your boss's reaction. Far better to go for compromise.
- Point out that part-timers, flexi-timers and job sharers are often more conscientious than full-timers. Companies where part-time work is established report an increase in commitment.
- Put together a package of literature (from addresses at end of book) which points out the advantages of flexible working. New Ways to Work (NWW) produce a range which also gives examples of how part-time jobs or job sharing operate.
- Back this up with a written summary of how you see your arrangement working. Make sure your planned schedule is realistic and anticipate pitfalls so you can answer objections.
- Talk to women in similar jobs who have re-negotiated their hours. If you don't know anyone, NWW may be able to help with contacts. The personnel officer and union representative should also be able to offer advice.
- Once you get down to the finer details of drawing up a new contract, remember that *you must work more than 16 hours a week for your full-time rights to be protected in law*. You should also find out how your pension will be affected.

Jacqui Bailey is an editorial director in a publishing company where part-time working among senior staff has been established for some time. But Jacqui didn't feel confident enough to re-negotiate her hours until after the birth of her second child. By then she'd proved to herself and her company that she *could* handle the demands of work and family, but she also felt very strongly that she did not want to go back full time.

Before she went on maternity leave Jacqui sounded out her immediate boss, who works four days in the office, plus a half day at home, about how it suited her, and proposed the same arrangement for herself. Her boss recommended it as a good compromise. Jacqui was concerned that the managing director would not accept two senior staff being absent on Fridays. 'But I've been with the company for 12 years and I was fairly confident about what I was asking for,' she says.

She prepared to counter any objections by pointing out that since she and her boss attended most meetings together, it could pose problems if there were two days of the week when they were unavailable. She was prepared to compromise, but she didn't have to.

Museum curator Naomi Joshi hatched the idea for her job share when she was expecting her first baby, Emily, now six. She was ready to do battle, as it was then rare for curators at the Victoria and Albert Museum to work part time.

Naomi prepared her ground by finding a suitable person within her department to share with. (One advantage of job sharing is that you don't have to negotiate alone!) They compiled a brief summary of how the share could work in practice, with a leaflet pointing out the pluses of job sharing for employers.

BEWARE LOSING YOUR JOB PROTECTION

Part-time working comes in many different guises: job sharing, flexi-time and some employers are now organising term-time working or school hour shifts. But whatever the name, all these arrangements are subject to our employment laws. For example, term-time working may be convenient, but if each holiday is counted as a break in service, it is impossible to build up enough continuous employment to qualify for job protection. *Unless your contract actually specifies that holidays do not constitute a break in service, workers can be sacked at any time.*

If you return to work on a more flexible basis, while not strictly part time, make sure your contract doesn't turn you, in effect, into a part-timer with limited rights. *If you split a 30-hour week as a job share, each of you will only be regarded in law as a part-timer doing 15 hours each.* Try to have the contract extended for two hours. Unfortunately, straightforward part-time workers are very vulnerable—see under Working part time below.

Also, make sure you are fully informed about the effects a change of working pattern will have on your pension and other job benefits before you commit yourself.

'I've no doubt that employing part-timers has its advantages for the employer,' says Naomi. 'With a job share, they get two people for the price of one.' If the museum hadn't agreed she would have left, although she didn't say so. 'But our boss was very supportive. He told us to write up our case and took it to the head of personnel who agreed straight away.'

Naomi has since been promoted to head of the Education Department of the Theatre Museum in Covent Garden (part of the V & A), while she was pregnant with her second child, Jack, proving that going part time doesn't always mean your career has to suffer!

What Are the Options?

Flexi-time

Flexi-time is a good compromise for women with school age children who want to put in an eight-hour day, but want to determine when they start and finish. Choosing to work 10–6 or 8–4, for example, cuts down the amount of pre- and post-school care you need to arrange, while not drastically altering your work schedule. You can still enjoy normal full-time benefits, including the salary and promotion opportunities.

Drawbacks: you still have the school holiday problem. Also, most employers who offer flexi-time contracts insist that all staff are present at a 'core' time of day, usually 10–4, so that office life is not disrupted by absences. Nervous employers may insist that once staff have chosen their hours they must stick to them, which makes rather a mockery of the term 'flexible' working. However, many flexi-time employees can mix their hours with a certain amount of homeworking, or work extra hours one week for time off in lieu the next.

Isobel Macdonald Davies is a statistician at the Office of Population Census and Surveys in central London. She has two children, Sandy, aged five, and Iona, 20 months. 'I worked 9–5 until my second child was born, then I felt I wanted more flexibility. A flexi-time system is available to everyone in the Civil Service, and people can work anytime between 7.30 am and 10.30 pm, with a core time of 10.30 am until 3.30 pm. I probably make maximum use of the system, but I'm not the only one who does, and I think that helps. I'm fortunate to work with many other working mothers, which means there is much more give and take between colleagues.

'I am required to work a total of 36 hours per week, which are "totted up" at the end of each month. I can distribute these as I choose. At the moment I work four days a week (three of which are eight hours) in term time. I am the major earner in our family and my husband is a teacher, so he can look after the children in the holidays, and I can work five long days. Half terms give me a chance to catch up on hours if necessary.

'Sometimes I have to make a decision about missing meetings; although I do come in to work very early on one day a week (7.30 am –6.30 pm), colleagues may want to get a meeting underway early on another day, when I start work later. But I think it helps that the office needs my skills, and that I am sufficiently senior. Speaking as a manager, employers have to be hard-headed and look at what staff produce at the end of each day. If they are happy, the work is better. That means being flexible with the work time, and not having a nine-to-five, bowler hat and umbrella attitude.'

Term-time working

Choosing to work only during term time can be a happy solution to the holiday childcare problem for mothers of school age children. Your salary is adjusted to take account of your unpaid leave, usually around ten weeks per year, but make sure your contract specifies your full terms and conditions of employment, which should be comparable to full-time employees but calculated on a pro rata basis.

Drawbacks: working in term time only is not really on for senior decision makers—business can't stop just because the kids have broken up—but it is an arrangement which suits professionals with specialist skills, where absences can be covered by rescheduling work. Some employers take on temporary replacements such as students on vacation or temporary staff from a pool of reserves on nil-hours contracts. The organisation New Ways to Work has more information on this increasingly popular form of flexible working.

Jenny Groves is a consultant pharmacist for the Boots company based in Essex. She has two sons, aged 14 and 11. 'My children had said since they were small that they didn't want to be looked after by anyone else, so I respected their wishes and only worked on and off part time. Boots regarded it as continuous employment, so three years ago I was able to start a "Flexible Parent Contract" —I was the first pharmacist in the company to do so.

'This contract entitles me to 14 weeks off a year during school holidays, made up of four weeks paid and the rest unpaid leave. Occasional days are thrown in too. Every employee is graded and paid hourly, regardless of whether they are full or part time, so I don't lose out that way. The scheme suits me perfectly and I would recommend it to anyone in a similar situation.

'I work Mondays and Saturdays full time, and 9.15 am–2.45 Tuesdays, Wednesdays and Thursdays. Now the children stay at school longer I can extend my hours—the scheme is flexible like that, but I can still be there for them in the holidays. The idea behind the contract is that it gives you the chance to get back into the swing of work, and I have been assured that when the right management promotion comes along, being part time won't hurt my chances.'

Job share

Job sharing presents a chance to do half a 'real job' with all the promotion prospects, perks and pay rises which go with it, and the employer gets two well-qualified people for the price of one. The division of hours and work patterns in a job share can vary: mothers with young babies often opt for two or three full days a week to consolidate childcare cover. Those with school age children may prefer working mornings only, while in contrast some job sharers arrange to work alternate weeks so they can really get their teeth into 40-hour stints of work. A word of caution: job sharers should ensure that they each work a minimum of 16 hours to retain employment rights and company benefits.

If you've found the ideal person with whom to job share, it's a good idea to approach your employer together, or to apply for a new post as a team. It's important for there to be good understanding and trust between two sharers. If one partner suspects the other is trying to expose their weakness in an attempt to climb the promotion ladder the relationship will never work. Job sharing is a mutually beneficial arrangement and over-ambitious behaviour is self-defeating.

Nicky Creed is Public Affairs Manager with the National Trust's Southern Region in Surrey. She has two children, aged three and one. 'I joined the National Trust seven years ago, and I think my being here this long definitely helped my case. I had often joked with my assistant that when we started our families we should job share. We had children at about the same time, so we decided to approach the Trust together and they agreed, but I don't think they would have considered it unless it suited them to keep on two relatively well-experienced people.

'We both do three days a week each—that's a rigid agreement unless one of us has a crisis at home. We try to have at least half a day in the office together. Because the job is a senior manager's, we found it more effective to split it into sections. I deal with some areas, my partner with others. It's a lot more effective this way as we each have different strengths and weaknesses. We have also divided up the staff in our department so that they are responsible to one or the other of us, so that encouragement or reprimand comes from the same designated person. The most important person is our very efficient secretary who liaises between us.

'I do think that with a job share you have to work extra hours to get the same job satisfaction as you did full time. Mine is a very interesting and challenging job, but if I didn't devote some of my own time too then it wouldn't be as rewarding.'

Working part time

At first glance, working on a purely part-time basis (for part of the week or day) seems an ideal option for a working mother. Britain has the largest number of part-time workers in the EC—they now make up 25% of the working population—and eight out of ten of those part-timers are women. However, current employment legislation means that there are some serious disadvantages which you should consider carefully before cutting back on your hours. **Drawbacks:** working part time gives you more time with your children, but far fewer rights than full-time workers. There are a few privileged part-timers, with valuable skills, who have been able to dictate their own terms after maternity leave. But the vast majority of women who return to part-time work after having children are returning to low wages, poor prospects and a lack of job security. The Low Pay Unit estimate that four out of five part-timers now earn less than the EC 'decency threshold' of around £3.30 an hour (in 1992).

The nature of the work has a lot to do with this. Ninety per cent of part-timers are in jobs which have always paid badly. Part-timers are less likely to get bonuses, premium paid overtime or to take on jobs with more responsibility. Some employers hold down hours, pay or both in order to keep the wages of individual employees below the £46 a week National Insurance threshold —saving themselves expense but depriving the part-timer of entitlement to state benefits.

While the majority of employment protection rights (such as redundancy pay, protection from unfair dismissal and the right to return after maternity leave) have to be 'earned' by a service qualification of two years, part-timers working between eight and 16 hours a week have to put in five years before they qualify. Those who work less than eight hours a week have no employment protection rights whatsoever.

The EC's proposed directive on 'atypical' workers, i.e. those with more flexible working arrangements, would give all those working over eight hours a week equal employment rights with full-time workers. There is a shift throughout the EC towards more flexible working, with an increase in homeworking predicted. It is largely women who will do this 'atypical' work, and legislation is needed to counterbalance the disadvantages they face in the single European market. But so far, the UK has blocked this directive.

However, some professions are now recognising the need to upgrade part-time opportunities in order to retain female skills; in particular the legal profession. Some large companies, including retail chains and banks, are now beginning to offer part-time jobs with pro rata benefits and career opportunities (see Chapter 13 for examples).

Nicola Newman works part time as Publicity Officer for Shell's Better Britain Campaign in Birmingham. Her daughter Josephine is two. 'I didn't have the option of returning to my previous full-time job in executive recruitment because I had worked for that employer for less than two years. However, while we wouldn't have starved if I'd stayed at home with Josephine, I wanted to do some kind of work for the status and an income for myself.

'When Josephine was three months old I set up my own recruitment company and worked from home. I gave myself two days a week, and found a wonderful childminder through the Social Services. Working from home certainly proved lucrative for a while, but during the summer, when demand for staff is low, I didn't have any work at all. By the autumn I had decided to start applying for part-time jobs so I could spend some time with Josephine, but I was determined not to accept any old job for the sake of it—this had to be a *real* job. I was prepared to lower my sights financially, but not professionally.

'Working for the Shell environmental campaign suits me perfectly. I negotiated three days a week, 9.30 am–5 pm so I could collect Josephine, on the understanding that I'd take short lunch breaks. My employer's only stipulation is that I work a minimum of 21 hours. My colleagues are very good about not ringing on my days off, and they will deal with anything urgent rather than leave a crisis brewing for my return.

'My holiday is pro rata, but I have all the sickness benefits of a full-time employee. I think I've proved to them that part time can work and the job will grow with me. My confidence in myself has grown and my relationship with Josephine has changed. It's not as intense, and perhaps I'm less patient with her, but that may be a good thing. I was far too indulgent before! On my third working day I do a child-swap with a friend who's also a part-timer, and I look after her daughter on one of my days off. It works very well.'

Working from home

New technology—computers, word processors, fax machines and electronic mail—all make it possible for workers in a wide variety of jobs to operate effectively without having to travel in to an office. 'Telecommuting' is becoming increasingly feasible and more organisations are employing homeworkers, many of them women who want to do a full-time job and still be at home for their children at the crucial times of day.

Drawbacks: pay tends to be less than for work done in the office, and may vary depending on the work-load. Remember that you will have increased heating and electricity bills, too. Before undertaking to work from home you should ensure you are not being excluded from existing wage agreements with your employer, and for employees who work only from home there is often little chance of promotion. Other disadvantages are those of the freelancer (see Freelance). As a homeworker you may feel isolated from colleagues, and may have to concentrate hard not to be distracted by huge piles of ironing. You will still need some sort of childcare, unless your baby is tiny and obligingly sleeps for large chunks of the working day.

RETRAINING FOR PART-TIME WORK—A GUIDE TO THE BEST JOBS

Cutting down the hours of your present job in order to manage family commitment might well lose you employment protection and much of the challenge and responsibility you previously enjoyed. If you'd like to have more time for the children now and also later when they start school, why not make some long-term plans to change your career rather than cut it back to the bone? You could use some of your time while the children are very young to retrain for a more absorbing part-time career which can be moulded round a school timetable. Many jobs are part time by their very nature, so the quality of work is higher. The following examples take no longer than two years to qualify for, and many take less.

Tourist Guide
Training: the majority of tourist boards run their own courses in the evening and at weekends. These can last from six months to two years. However, they are not cheap (£500 rising to over £1,500 in London). There is competition for places and a stringent entry test. It helps to have a foreign language, although that's not essential. Or you could become a guide in a stately home (most give on-the-job training) but there are long waiting lists.
Salary: from £90 a day for a Blue Badge guide and £55 a day for a stately home guide.
Contact: The Guild of Guide Lecturers, 2 Bridge Street, London SW1A 2JR (Tel: 071-839 7438); also local tourist boards and stately homes.

Market Researcher
This doesn't necessarily mean standing in the street with a clipboard. You can work from home, or there are other openings on the executive side.
Training: in theory you don't need formal training although it is now common to have a degree, a business studies qualification or the year-long diploma of the Market Research Society. This can either be studied for at home or through a local further education college. The society, which can put you in touch with companies seeking researchers via its free booklet, has an education department which runs general courses and refresher seminars.
Contact: Market Research Society (Tel: 071-490 4911).

Librarian
Training: The Library Association offers careers advice for anyone wanting to work in a library. It also endorses a number of post-

graduate polytechnic courses, the minimum of which is one year. Librarianship can also lead to more specialised work for private companies. The need for shift work makes it ideal for part-timers.
Salary: from £12,000 full time.
Contact: The Library Association (Tel: 071-636 7543).

Social Work

More mature employees are being encouraged to take up part-time social work, even if they haven't worked in the field before, according to the Central Council for Education and Training in Social Work.
Training: there is now a two-year social work diploma which can be taken at FE colleges. However, applicants must have done some sort of related voluntary work. Previous skills which might help you get into social work include nursing, teaching, welfare work or bringing up your family.
Salary: from £12,000.
Contact: Central Council for Education and Training in Social Work (Tel: 071-278 2455).

Horticulture

Training: according to the Institute of Horticulture, you do not need formal training for basic levels, such as working in a garden centre, where on-the-job training will be given. However, to progress higher (for example into garden design) you need further training, and there is quite a variety available. Examples include the part time City and Guilds qualification in horticulture (two years) and some full time national diploma courses and also degrees. There's often a demand for temporary staff at garden centres, which suits part-timers, and if you set up in garden design yourself you are a free agent.
Salary: £3 plus per hour.
Contact: The Institute of Horticulture, PO Box 313, 80 Vincent Square, London SW1P 2PE (please send an sae for information).

Kitchen Design

Training: some kitchen companies, such as Kitchen Direct and Moben, offer in-house training to would-be designers, even if they have never worked in the field before. 'The experience of a woman who understands exactly how a kitchen should be laid out is just as valuable,' says spokeswoman Tina Hancox. The training courses last around three months and take place during the day, but designers then usually work evenings when their clients are at home.
Salary: from £15,000, although some of this is based on commission. (NB there is selling involved, although designers don't make cold calls.)
Contact: Kitchens Direct (Tel: 061-872 2422); also local kitchen firms.

Some homeworkers are regarded as self-employed, and as such have to be responsible for paying their own NI contributions and filling in tax returns. If you are still an employee of a company you should be entitled to full rights. The organisation Ownbase (see page 207) can provide more information.

Karina Beeke is senior engineer at BBC Transmission in the Midlands. She has one daughter, Hannah, who is 16 months old. 'I had been working for the BBC for seven years before taking maternity leave, so I think my length of service helped when it came to asking for a homeworking arrangement. I had always known I wouldn't want to leave a small child full time, so when I became pregnant I approached my section head with the idea. I made notes on how I thought it would work in practice; working full time, although not simply nine to five. He took the idea to more senior management and they came back with a formal proposal, which included such things as "core hours" when I would be available by phone, and the number of times I would go into the office to talk to my section head. After some thought I decided it would be easier if I went into the office for a set couple of mornings a week, and so Hannah goes to a local creche then. Sometimes, when I have to attend meetings and conferences, my mother will have her. My mother-in-law lives near London, which is useful if there are meetings down there.

'My job tends to be more theoretical, giving out advice and computer modelling rather than hands-on. Working from home seemed to be the natural solution; if I had to do a lot of site-work at transmitter stations then it wouldn't be possible. Homeworking hasn't meant I've lost touch with the other engineers. The BBC has provided me with a computer, printer and fax and I have a chargecard for all my business calls.

'I don't get distracted being at home; when I get up on Monday morning it's definitely the start of a working week. The housework gets ignored because, quite simply, my job is far more interesting! I make sure Hannah is engrossed in her toys before I start making my important calls; she sleeps in the afternoon and I have a block of time then, and after she has gone to bed for the night. I do have to work some weekends to catch up, but that would have happened anyway, and it's so much easier having your computer at home!

'In fact, so far homeworking hasn't done my career any harm at all. If anything I am representing the BBC more than I was before I had Hannah. I certainly haven't been pushed into a backwater and my salary is unaffected, although if I applied for promotion I would probably be asked to return to the office full time because those jobs are not suited to homeworking.'

Freelance/self-employed

The major advantage of being freelance (and it's a life that suits many professions from PRs to interior designers) is your freedom —to work when and for whom you like. You can take on work when it suits you, for example during term time, and become 'unavailable' during the holidays.

Drawbacks: lack of financial security and sole responsibility for the work are the obvious disadvantages; but don't forget that working for yourself can be lonely and hard on your confidence on occasions, so you need to be the resilient type. You must keep your accounts well organised, paying your own tax, insurance and NI contributions. If your turnover is less than £10,000 a year you can keep the tax man satisfied by submitting a 'three line account' showing turnover, expenditure and profit, but if things are more complicated you will need an accountant who knows about small businesses (and has small fees to match!). There are several agencies which offer expert help to small businesses (see page 209); you may also be eligible for an Enterprise Allowance, so contact your local Training and Enterprise Council (TEC) who will give free advice. See also Chapter 12, under Home-based business, for other points to consider.

Jane Grant runs her own PR consultancy, PR Support, from her home in Warwick. She has two children aged 11 and nine. 'I have worked since my daughter was a month old, but I was married then, so it was only really for pocket money, not out of financial necessity as now. When I left my husband, the bank manager warned me that "things couldn't go on like this", and told me I must take responsibility for my own income. I took the first job I was offered, heading a PR department of a local company. I thought it was well paid considering I'd had a career break, but I couldn't cope with the childcare! I got through two nannies in six months. I felt really guilty; I didn't get home until 7.30 pm each night, so I couldn't oversee the children's homework. I was anxious that things weren't being done to my standards. It was a huge wrench giving up my role as prime carer, let alone having to pay someone else to ferry the children from school, to friends, to ballet.

'So after six months I started PR Support, taking one client with me. I now have a copywriter and a book-keeper working for me part time, and a typist who comes in to help. I also took on a cleaning lady who comes in once a fortnight for a whole day and cleans the house from top to bottom. The children help too, making their beds and laying the table.

'I've gained the flexibility to run my own day, and manage my own diary—I don't have to be "seen doing things" and I can be around for the children when they need me. But I do try to be disciplined to avoid distractions—I turn on the computer at 9 am and answer the phone with the company name from then on. My clients don't seem to have a problem with my being home-based. I think attitudes are changing—business doesn't need to be all glitz and big boardrooms, clients have been ripped off for so long by PR agencies with big retainers. I can be far more competitive.'

CHAPTER 12

After the Break: Returning, Refreshing and Retraining Opportunities; How to Make a Fresh Start

When you decide to go back to work after running a home and bringing up children for several years, you are not at your most confident. You feel out of date and out of touch, and wonder if you have anything to offer.

Well, you'd be surprised.

You may feel you're more familiar with a food rather than word processor, but you are still a highly desirable commodity, and that's an official fact. Women returning to work after a break make good employees; they are motivated, reliable, mature, able to manage time effectively, deal with finances and cope with emergencies. The fact that they have been running a home and managing children and family proves their competence.

Sadly, these valuable skills have long been undervalued in 'the workplace', which doesn't help women returners to realise that they often have far more to offer than school leavers, whose numbers are dwindling anyway. But the future looks promising, as more employers realise they must become women-friendly to survive these major demographic changes. Even more encouraging are the efforts now being made to officially recognise women's domestic or unpaid skills and to make them count towards a formal vocational qualification.

A study to analyse the range and level of competence acquired from managing a home and family is currently being undertaken by the Employment Department. A forerunner to this national project was carried out by Birmingham City Council, which measured the 'Administration, Business and Commercial' (ABC) competence of a small group of 'housewives' who had decided to enter Employment Training. The initial findings make interesting reading: before gloomily writing off your time spent at home with the children, you might like to consider the following:

- Women carrying out normal household clerical tasks (paying and filing bills, answering letters, dealing with banks and building societies) were likely to have acquired up to 50% of the range of competence required for an ABC (NVQ) Levels I/II Award.

• Some women achieved even more than 50% when their unpaid work in the community and volunteering were taken into account.

• When measured against required levels of competence in management and supervision, some women reached standards recommended for industry.

So, when you are thinking about returning to work, remember that your domestic experience is valuable and can be made to count towards many vocational qualifications. You may even be able to talk yourself straight into a job, particularly if you have kept up work contacts while being a full-time mum. However, the majority of women, regardless of the jobs they did before having children, feel a shadow of their former, confident selves and need some kind of formal course or further training to ease themselves back into full-time work. There is certainly a lot of help available—at first sight, rather too much!

A mother who is feeling distinctly unsure of herself and what she wants to do after several years out of paid work can find the choice bewildering. Likewise the woman who is unhappy and demoralised in her current job, and wishes to improve her educational or vocational qualifications to further her career.

This chapter explores the options available so you can get a clearer idea of how you want to proceed. The thoughts and advice from women who took up various challenges will help you see just what can be achieved, and should help you decide if a course of action is right for you. You will find useful addresses and further information sources on page 207–209.

The Best Place to Start—Confidence Building

In the face of all the new chances, choices and shiny new schemes, the first major decision for women at home or work who want to equip themselves for change is simply 'where do I start?'

'With yourself', comes the advice from training consultant Georgina Corscadden. 'It's impossible to make the right career decision unless you understand your strengths and weaknesses, and can identify and tackle the obstacles in the way of personal fulfilment. You also must like and respect yourself, too, otherwise you make other people regard you negatively.'

Georgina has found that the needs of women returners and career changers often overlap, so she has designed an intensive one-day course to tackle the root of the common problems. Both groups feel unsatisfied with their current situation, but lack the confidence and self-esteem to see clearly what they want, and what they are capable of. Each share an uncanny knack of forgetting or dismissing the important skills they already possess.

'I call it the "Time Lock" effect,' explains Georgina. 'Both groups disregard the past; returners simply wipe out their working experience before children, while the changers speak of it all in negative terms. I've seen an ex-senior barrister, near to tears, stand up and tell one astonished group that she hadn't any skills. Also, women, generally, suffer from an innate honesty which stops them mentioning any achievements they think are not strictly relevant. One course had been running nearly three hours before one woman "admitted" that she had a private pilot's licence!'

Through group exercises, Georgina promotes self-awareness and confidence; women are encouraged to sift through their entire life experiences in order to list achievements of all kinds, which in turn leads to a clearer identification of their individual skills and potential.

'Committing things to paper—for example, listing strengths and weaknesses—often gives you a new insight,' advises Georgina, 'although without objective support, women will always list far more weaknesses!' By the end of the day, Georgina aims to have helped each group member to feel better about herself and have a clear objective to be achieved within a time limit.

Examining your strengths and weaknesses

Sitting down alone, examining your strengths and weaknesses has its pitfalls, of course. If you start from a basis of low confidence, the exercise will be self-defeating. Observations from friends, even casual acquaintances, can be extremely illuminating. A less stark way of doing this is to follow Georgina's 'Life in the Day' exercise with a friend. Sit down together over a coffee while you condense your general experiences into an 'average day', describing all the things you do, using the day as a time frame. Your friend should sit with a sheet of paper divided into 'Strengths and Weaknesses', and fill in the qualities expressed while you talk about your various activities. She should not interrupt, except to draw you out when necessary.

THE SIGNPOST CHART

One of the exercises most central to Georgina's course is done
individually and committed 'privately' to paper, as many women
feel intimidated at the thought of sharing intimate experiences with
the rest of the group. It's ideal to do by yourself at home, provided
you are as honest as possible and include as many examples as you
possibly can, however trivial they seem.

Divide a sheet of A4 paper into four vertical columns under the
headings ROLES, JOBS, EXPERIENCES and SKILLS. Taking each
column in turn, read the following and complete the first three
before drawing everything together under SKILLS.

ROLES: under this heading write down *all* your different roles—
think as broadly as possible—you may find after some time at home
with children that wife and mother are the only ones you can
remember. Try harder—what happened to your personal identity?

JOBS: write down all the jobs, paid or unpaid, which you have ever
held in your life—from papergirl onwards if necessary. Include all
the unofficial posts you've held while at home, bringing up children:
caterer, financial planner, supervisor etc.

EXPERIENCES: This is the broadest category of all—include every
experience you have had, major or minor. Having a baby, doing
an evening course, fixing the car, organising a party, learning to
drive, taking an exam, coping with bereavement, getting a bottle
bank installed at your local supermarket.

SKILLS: Drawing together what you have gained from various
roles, jobs and experiences, write down all the skills you have
developed. What you are able to write here should act as a signpost
to the type of job you would most enjoy and do well at. What is
so valuable about this exercise, apart from giving you a concrete
starting point, is that it can throw up some surprises and challenges.
Have you, former bank clerk, spent most of your time at home
fixing things, enjoyed putting up shelves and discovering you actually enjoy doing minor repairs to the car? Or have you, previously
timid secretary, found new confidence as a mother and active, voci-
ferous PTA member. Look at that skills column—perhaps you
should consider a more organisational role.

When you're feeling more confident, cast your net wider. 'Ask as many different types of people as possible—male, female, old, young, those in and out of work—what they think are your good points,' advises business psychologist Alison Hardingham. 'You'll be surprised at how many things you take for granted about yourself, that other people admire or recognise as plus points.'

Alison also stresses the importance of using people as well as books as research sources for a possible new career. 'People love talking about themselves. "Interview" them about the work they do, in detail. Even if you're feeling out of touch as a mum with young children, you will have access to a wide network of useful people in a variety of jobs. Think about all the partners and friends of the other mums in your playgroup, for example.'

Overcoming the Barriers

What about the everyday, practical obstacles to 'Mum' returning to paid employment? As the lynchpin of the family, you can probably quote a string of 'But what abouts' (the children/granny/the dog), all of which seem to prevent you getting back to work. Don't despair—make another list of these 'restrictions' and look at them objectively. Decide which are genuine obstacles to tackle, and which are just excuses. 'The dog needs a daily walk' is not good enough—what about early morning or evening? Or what about asking a neighbour?

The various types of childcare are examined in Chapters 2–7. If you're worried about leaving your children, refer back to the reassuring advice from child psychologists on pages 22–23. It's natural to feel a bit wobbly yourself—you are not the first, nor will you be the last, mum to ring up the childminder in tears on your first day back at work!

Childcare may not be your only problem—caring for elderly relations is a major obstacle to many women returning to work. One in nine of all full-time workers and one in six of all part-time workers are carers. Problems are increasing as the population ages. The office workers' research and information organisation, City Centre, offers the following advice on 'eldercare' in their useful information pack *Women: Returning to Work*.

CARING FOR THE ELDERLY

Care at home
Home helps: Social Services can provide someone who comes in to visit and do light work for an elderly person, such as shopping or preparing a meal. You might be charged a small amount but the service is generally free.

Meals on wheels: many local authorities have cut this valuable service, but where it exists a hot meal is delivered once a day to elderly people unable to prepare food themselves.

Some Social Services departments and some charities: Crossroads (see page 207 for address) will offer respite care (someone to sit with an elderly person, freeing the carer for a few hours). Respite care can also mean taking the relative into a residential home for a few days.

Health visitors and district nurses: you can sometimes get fairly regular visits from health visitors and district nurses to help with an elderly person's care, particularly personal hygiene. Contact the person's doctor.

Private care at home
Nurse: these can be found through nursing agencies, health visitors, GPs, residential homes (staff wanting more work), the local paper or word of mouth. Private nurses are expensive and will usually cost from £6–£8 an hour.

Unqualified carer: these can be found through agencies dealing with home helps and au pairs, or through health visitors, GPs, the local press or word of mouth. Cost will be around £3 an hour.

Companions: a companion will not normally perform nursing duties, but will provide some help and ensure someone is there at certain times of the day. Can be found through the same channels as unqualified carers (above) and will cost around £2–£4 an hour.

Day centres
These are run by Social Services or privately (addresses are held by Social Services departments) or by charities (Age Concern has 250 over the country). Some local authorities provide transport. Some centres will only take people for one or two days a week.

Luncheon clubs
If your relative is fairly mobile but you worry about their ability to have a proper meal in the daytime, Social Services run luncheon clubs which provide food and sometimes social activities (see page 207 for addresses).

Returning/Refreshing

If you want to brush up your existing office skills and update your experience, there is now a wealth of short courses aimed at returners all over the country. Those offered by your local College of Further Education or Adult Education Institute are inexpensive and should be designed to fit in with family commitments. While some courses emphasise general confidence building and 'getting back in touch', others are more strongly vocational and are designed to familiarise women with modern technology with a view to finding a specific office job.

Some returners' courses offer work placements, with the possibility of employment at the end. Hertfordshire management consultants Dow Stoker, who specialise in training women returners, offer free courses to local women, sponsored by Hertfordshire Technical College. Along with general confidence building, interview techniques and assertiveness training, potential returners can benefit from hands-on experience.

For Gill Page, 41, this opportunity resulted in a job offer from local employers Peter Dominic. Former secretary Gill, whose three children are now teenagers, spent six weeks on part-time placement at the company's head office as part of the Dow Stoker course.

'I didn't feel very much was expected of me, so I relaxed and soaked it all up. Everyone was very friendly and patient; so much had changed it took some getting used to! I was able to learn how to use the computer, I sat in on the switchboard, on reception and in the personnel department. It all helped me decide that I would prefer to work directly with people, perhaps in reception or personnel.'

The management spotted her potential and asked her to join the personnel department full time: in order to fulfil family commitments Jill negotiated a job share—which was a first for Peter Dominic, too!

Return to Learning

While retraining to update office skills is often the first choice for women, you should take your time deciding before you beat the traditionally female path back to work. Many colleges also offer broader based 'Return to Study' or 'Return to Learning' courses which are aimed at women who have been away from either education or work for a period of time and wish to explore a variety of new options.

One of the major benefits of any course is the stimulation and support other women will provide. Returners' courses tend to attract an interesting cross-section of the community both in age and background. Another advantage of the broad-based course is that any woman who is feeling confused about the future and unsure of herself is exposed to new and challenging career options while sharpening up her mind generally.

For example, the Women's Return to Study Course offered by the North West London (NWL) Regional College aims to build confidence and develop new and existing skills. Subjects studied include English, maths and science, with some assertiveness training and careers guidance. The overall aim is to encourage women to go on to further study, although not always in the areas they might traditionally expect.

Jane Serafy-Nafis left her job as a beauty consultant when she had her son Kayvan in 1986. She ventured on to NWL's Return to Study course three years later, with no particular aim in mind. Now, aged 30, she has completed one of the most interesting new courses offered at the college, a two-year, part-time Higher National Certificate in Building Services Engineering (Refrigeration and Air Conditioning).

'I thought I was just going to college for six weeks, which might be interesting. I had no intention of going on to further study,' says Jane, who admits she hated school and left at 16 with one O level. 'But the Return to Study course was great fun, with all sorts of women who got on really well. I began to enjoy the experience of learning—even tackling maths, which I used to hate.'

Jane admits she was astonished, then intrigued when the tutors suggested that she go on to study engineering. Cathy Walsh, Co-ordinator for Equal Opportunities, was instrumental in setting up the course. 'The construction industry should not be regarded exclusively as a male domain, and we wanted to encourage women to consider training for this well-paid work,' says Cathy.

Jane admits Cathy's unfailing support and enthusiasm helped her through difficult patches. 'Walking into a classroom of 25 men was rather frightening at first, now I have greater confidence with large groups of men. The course is theory-based, and I had no trouble holding my own, even with the maths. On another level, I've developed a thirst for knowledge which has completely changed me, I no longer feel I'm just drifting through life.'

New Technology Training

It's worth remembering that information technology skills have an application in a variety of fields. Even if you have no intention of ending up back in an office, you may find them a useful string to your bow. Many colleges and training centres run women-only courses in computing. For a list of courses contact Microsystems or the Pepperell Unit (see page 207 for addresses). Other organisations are also running similar courses, for example 'Women and Technology' for women over 25, which is geared towards industry and business and is sponsored by companies who provide work experience. It is run at Drake House (see page 208).

If, like many women, you are well qualified and experienced in office skills but feel unsure of your ability to cope with new technology, the best kind of courses to look for are those which incorporate flexible learning, where the teaching is tailored to the needs and ability level of the women who apply.

Cambridge Regional College (CRC) offers a good example, designed to attract refreshers and returners of varying ages and experience. 'Office Skills for the 90s' can cater for those women without any previous office training, alongside the more qualified but rusty returners. Running for ten weeks, nine hours a week, the course costs around £85.

Changing direction

It's not often you find a former horticulturalist among those studying office skills. Lee Steele, 32, has a prestigious roof garden in London's Covent Garden to her credit, among many others. While taking time out to bring up Jake, five, and Ross, two, she organised several successful fund-raising art exhibitions on a voluntary basis and discovered it was a direction she wished to pursue professionally.

'I went along for a couple of part-time jobs in galleries,' says Lee, 'but discovered despite my exhibition experience I needed office skills. Gallery assistants have to handle a lot of administrative work, particularly using computers.'

Lee decided against a private word processing training course on the advice of a friend in the Cambridge Careers office, who encouraged her to think long term, and recommended the more flexible option offered at CRC.

'I'm not good at learning things parrot fashion,' admits Lee, 'but I found learning to type surprisingly easy, although I'm still very slow. What is useful about the course is that you can opt for extra lessons in areas of weakness, for a nominal fee. I found the business studies lessons particularly useful.' Lee plans to continue organising exhibitions on a voluntary basis, building up her new network of contacts. 'I'm lucky, I don't have to get a full-time job while the kids are still so young, so I don't have to rush into anything. But when something comes along, I'll be ready to snap it up.'

Learning Long Distance

If family responsibilities mean it would be difficult to get out to daytime, or even evening courses, or you don't have a convenient college nearby, distance learning is worth considering, even just for interest and stimulation. The fact you have made the effort will impress some employers when you finally return to work.

The Open University: no qualifications are needed to join and you can study at your own pace, in your own home with a tutor to guide you (by correspondence). If you have decided on a plan of action and know you need further qualifications, using your children's pre-school years to make a start means you are that much nearer to achieving your objective when you have more free time. Bear in mind, however, that an Open University degree takes twice as long to complete as an ordinary degree.

Alternatively, you could take a single-subject, shorter course with the OU Business School, for a Certificate of Course Completion. These include an eight-week Women into Management course, aimed at women returning to or entering management, and unemployed women.

The Open College provides short courses by correspondence, with some TV programmes. One course 'Women: the way ahead' is specially aimed at women returning to work.

The National Extension College has a variety of GCSEs, A-levels and learn new skill and training courses.

Flexi-study or **Open Learning** are packages offered by some Adult Education Institutes (AEI). They include study packs, cassettes, videos for learning at home or when you can fit it in at an open learning centre,.

Correspondence courses are often advertised widely, but beware, not all are reputable. For a list of accredited colleges contact the Council for the Accreditation of Correspondence Colleges (address on page 208).

Coming back to life

Philippa Brown, who is 29 and has four-year-old twin boys and a 12-year-old son, chose the Open University because she could work her course round her children. Ten years ago she did a BA in English at university, now she is highly motivated by the prospect of a career as a psychological counsellor. She crams ten hours of uninterrupted study into one day every week when the children go to her mother-in-law. Philippa's husband takes over childcare in the run-up to exams and essays, and when she goes away to the Open University's annual residential summer school. Because it's so easy for OU students to become isolated, they are encouraged to make contact with each other.

'I go to tutorials and see how the others are getting on,' says Philippa, 'to find out what their marks are like and so on. At first, I was a bit disappointed by the other students, they were mostly much older than me. But that feeling went completely once I got into the work, and the mixture of ages and attitudes turned out to be one of the most rewarding things about the course.'

Student mothers are no less prey to guilt than working women. When the pressure is on, Philippa admits to feeling bad: 'If an essay's due or an exam coming up, it's all-encompassing. Everything else goes out of the window. At times like that—when my eldest son has to get his own food and the twins are plonked in front of the telly and I'm shouting at everyone—yes, I do feel guilty.'

Enthusiasm and determination have carried her through the inevitable periods of flagging motivation. Studying is tiring and it can be emotionally draining, but Philippa still thinks it's all worth it. 'I was coming out of a tutorial and I felt I was meeting myself

again, that this person that I hadn't known for years was waking
up inside me. It was just like coming back to life.'

Deciding on a Change

Doing your homework thoroughly is vital when it comes to launch-
ing into a new career. You may feel determined not to go back to
the old job you had before children, but was it really the actual
work you disliked?

'Examine those rumblings of discontent very carefully,' advises
Alison Hardingham. 'You may find that you enjoyed your work,
but it was colleagues or general environment which was getting
you down.'

As part of Alison's professional management consultancy service
to firms, she offers careers assessments and counselling to staff in
need of direction. From experience she knows that the grass often
looks greener on the other side of the fence . . . if you don't look
too carefully.

'You must know as much as possible about the new career you
are contemplating, the day-to-day routine. Ask yourself some
tough questions—what really would be different from your previous job, or are you just swapping one desk for another? People
often have rather vague, even rather romantic ideas about alternative careers and are preparing to embark on four or five years
retraining without really knowing what their new life will entail.'

If you are absolutely sure you want a change, but don't know
what you want to do, private careers counselling can help, although
it can be expensive. Shop around before parting with any money.
There is plenty of choice in what has been a boom industry over
the past few years, and inevitably standards vary. Wherever possible, be guided by personal recommendation.

Counselling usually takes the form of an intensive one-day session, which combines the results of systematic personality analysis
and one-to-one counselling to produce a very detailed personal
career recommendation. Hidden talents often emerge, which can
set off fresh and exciting career possibilities.

Even if you haven't worked for many years you can still benefit
from professional careers counselling. George Summerfield, director of Careers Analysts, points out that many doubting women
returners have had their confidence boosted by their test results;

concrete written evidence that their intelligence remains. 'We can give objective proof that you do not lose your aptitude for certain types of career, even if you've spent 12 years bringing up a family.'

Running your own business

Change is not always welcome, of course. Redundancy can come as a real blow, particularly when you have re-established yourself in your career after having children. If you are very experienced, with plenty of contacts and enthusiasm, some business training could help you become successfully self-employed.

Lou Foreman, 46, was 'devastated' when she was made redundant from a job she loved. Lou, with a long and varied background in professional catering, had been restaurant supervisor at a leading Coventry hotel when it was sold, and she found herself out of work with a mortgage and two teenage sons to support.

At her age, lengthy retraining for a new career was not a viable option. 'Build on your experience,' came the sound advice from a friend who worked at the Coventry Business Centre. 'She told me I had what it takes to run my own business,' remembered Lou. 'I had confidence in my catering abilities, but found the thought of the VAT, wages and accounts terrifying.'

Like many areas of high unemployment, Coventry has developed a very go-ahead Careers Service to encourage new initiatives. The Business Centre is an independent consultancy attached to the service, and offers much-needed help for women like Lou who have to learn on their feet.

'I took over a franchise for a tourist restaurant with Coventry Cathedral; and for one morning a week the business centre sent their accountant to help me do the books. He was really patient, standing over me until I could do it all alone. In fact, his training gave me the confidence to train my son, who now runs my *second* business, a hot and cold food bar.'

Working from home

Running a business from home can be a very successful way of balancing work and family commitments, particularly once your children have started school. You may be able to use previously acquired skills, but you must do your research thoroughly first. Is there a market for your chosen product or service? It's also vital to take an honest look at yourself. Have you the personality to cope? You must be self-sufficient enough to be on your own during the day, and have plenty of confidence and lots of self-discipline. Get good business advice *before* committing yourself to anything (see addresses on page 209) and consider *all* the necessary formalities:

• Change of use of your home: don't run into problems with your local authority after you've got under way—contact them first if your work will substantially alter the character of your home or if it requires planning permission. Also check whether you will have to pay the business rate. If you have a mortgage, make sure the lender approves of using the property as a business base.

• Health and safety: contact your local Health and Safety office to make sure your work doesn't constitute a hazard.

• Type of business: see your solicitor for advice on whether to set up as a limited company or sole trader and how to register the name of your business.

• Income tax: if you're self-employed, notify the local tax office to assess how much you should pay. The Inland Revenue issues a free booklet *Starting In Business* explaining how tax is calculated, which business expenses can be offset against the bill and your liabilities as an employer.

• National Insurance: contact the Department of Social Security to find out how much you should pay. If you're employing others, you will have to pay national insurance and PAYE. See DSS leaflet *Self-employed? A guide to your NI contributions and social security benefits*.

• VAT: if your taxable turnover exceeds £36,600 a year you must register for VAT, unless you deal with goods which are partly or wholly zero rated. Contact your local Customs & Excise office for its booklet *Should I be registered for VAT?*

Samantha Bordell, a former textile designer, now works from home where she designs and makes greeting cards by hand. When her son Thomas was very young, she worked while he slept, now she employs a part-time nanny.

'I was already hankering for a change of direction when I became pregnant,' remembers Samantha, 'so I gave up full-time work completely. When Thomas was born I found my priorities changed. I stopped thinking of myself as a career woman and started thinking of ways to work from home so I could enjoy my baby as much as possible.'

Samantha sells her intricate and unusual cards mostly by mail order and is slowly expanding the business to the stage where she can employ skilled outworkers to make up the cards, leaving her free to concentrate on design. Her friend Jo Hunter, an accountant who also has a young son James, has joined her as business partner, responsible for the books and for investigating new outlets.

'Right now I want to keep things small, I'm just working to order. I haven't the time to build up a huge stock of cards. My outlay is minimal—I've found wholesalers who will let me have small amounts of ribbon, beads and so on. At this stage, most of the money I make is ploughed back into the business.'

Whatever you decide to do, persevere. A change of direction or a new beginning can only be healthy and positive. Just think how awful it would be to wake up aged 70 and look back on a life of missed opportunities.

CHAPTER 13
Companies Who Care: Some Positive Examples for the Future

This chapter looks at what some enlightened employers are already offering their working parents. If your company doesn't match up, you might like to recommend your personnel officer makes further investigation! This is not a comprehensive list, but provides a flavour of what is happening in a variety of areas, in both the public and private sectors.

The following examples of companies taking the lead with family-friendly employment practices, childcare provision and positive encouragement for women returners include American Express Europe Ltd, the winner of the 1991 *SHE*/Working Mothers Association Employer Award, and several finalists.

Robin Derrett, Manager of Employee Relations at American Express Europe Ltd, says that Amex make it a priority to support staff with their family and lifestyle needs, especially by being more flexible. Amex have also made an effort to help parents in the community, not just their own employees, by helping to fund Brighton Childcare Link. For the company, improving the quality of life for their employees makes good business sense. As Robin Derrett sums it up: 'You can't expect to get that extra 20% from your staff if you don't give a damn what happens to them outside working hours.'

AMERICAN EXPRESS EUROPE LIMITED
Based: Brighton
Number of employees: 2700 in Brighton area
Childcare
- A 50-place nursery has been set up near their Brighton headquarters in conjunction with a local childcare organisation, open to children aged three to five years from 7.30 am–6 pm.
- Supervised holiday playscheme for five–12 year olds.
- Amex has contributed more than £30,000 to the research, development and launch of UK Childcare Links, a new initiative which provides childcare 'resource and referral' services to local communities

nationwide. Brighton Childcare Link, the first of these, provides information on local facilities in the Brighton community.

Employment benefits

Around 20% of Brighton-based staff now work a variety of work patterns, including working from home, term-time contracts, teleworking and job sharing. There is also a career break option.

Future plans

• Amex is working towards expanding the nursery provision, and it is also supporting a local scheme to provide after-school care for older children.

OFFICE OF POPULATION, CENSUS AND SURVEYS (OPCS)
Based: London, Southport and Titchfield, Hants
Employees: 2500
Childcare

• Holiday playschemes for primary age children.

• Provision being worked on to allow out-of-hours childcare costs to be reimbursed (to allow attendance at evening meetings, weekend courses etc.).

• Leave (paid or unpaid) is available to cover school holidays or to look after sick children.

• Information on childcare available to employees.

Employment benefits

• In addition to standard Civil Service terms for maternity leave, OPCS staff can also take unpaid leave of 52 weeks. They can also choose the start date of paid maternity leave.

• Flexible working is available to full- and part-time staff. All arrangements are based on calendar months and allow a maximum of three days flexi-leave and three days 'credit' to be carried over, per month.

• Part-time work and job sharing available; equal promotion eligibility with full-timers.

• Career breaks, with return to the same grade.

• Homeworking.

• Management flexibility, such as long and short days, four-day weeks and extreme hours.

Future plans

• A survey is being drawn up to determine childcare needs, with the possibility of linking up with other government departments.

ELIDA GIBBS
Based: Leeds
Employees: 1200 (70% women)
Childcare

• Childminding link scheme set up in 1990, co-ordinated by a local authority childcare expert seconded to the company. The co-ordinator undertakes to find a childminder for employees' children in their own community, whether part-time, full-time or for after-school pick-up. The childminders are all registered with the local authority, and although still self-employed, have their insurance premiums and annual registration fee paid by the company. Employees can use this service before and during maternity leave.

• Beneficial rates for childminding—the company tops up fees as costs increase.

Employment benefits

• Flexi-time, part-time and, in some departments, homeworking contracts are available.

• Discretionary benefits for managers and assistant managers include maternity pay make-up scheme; a back payment to top up maternity leave pay to full pay is made on completion of six months' post-leave service; company benefits, such as car and private health scheme, can be retained throughout maternity leave, until and unless employee decides not to return; parent company Unilever operate a contact network to keep all senior maternity leavers in touch.

ALLIED DUNBAR ASSURANCE PLC

Based: Swindon plus nationwide branches

Employees: 2600

Childcare

• Use of company-based childcare co-ordinator (who previously worked for Childminding in Business! Ltd).

• Use of 50-place nursery based close to headquarters, and run by Kids Unlimited with priority given to Allied Dunbar employees. Eight full-time baby places.

• Link with childminding network. Minders are registered with local authority but vetted and monitored by company childcare co-ordinator. The company also pays their insurance and registration fees, plus a two-month retainer with a new child to ensure parents are satisfied. A back-up scheme operates with approved reserve minders taking over in case of illness. The company also operates a toys and equipment loan scheme.

Employment benefits

• Option of 52 weeks unpaid maternity leave in addition to statutory maternity leave.

• Contact during maternity cover through department managers and company news sheet.

• Part-time and flexi-time work, depending on needs of particular departments.

Future plans

• A holiday care scheme for employees' children.

LEICESTER CITY COUNCIL
Employees: 4230
Childcare
- Subsidised 45-place nursery. Sliding fee scale dependent on family income.
- Emergency childcare expenses reimbursed if incurred by extra work demands from council.

Employment benefits
- Improved maternity leave—18 weeks paid and 42 weeks unpaid regardless of amount of time employee has worked for the council.
- Ten days paternity leave.
- Adoption leave—as maternity leave without the period before the birth.
- Flexible working, including job share.
- Career break scheme, including retainer scheme for maintaining links while on maternity leave, and retraining scheme.
- Homeworking.
- Women's groups—monthly meetings to cover issues which specifically relate to women employees.
- Career counselling and appraisal scheme which runs across the whole authority, and operates an 'open door' policy with employee's manager.

Future plans (now being worked on)
- Childminding network
- Parental leave
- Holiday playscheme
- Term-time working

THE BOOTS COMPANY PLC
Based: nationwide, head office Nottingham
Employees: 76% workforce female
Childcare
- Boots-sponsored holiday playscheme in Nottingham (came about after pressure from a Working Mothers' Group set up at head office, who meet every couple of months to discuss relevant issues. The groups also produce a newspaper with advice and information which is sent to all mothers on the staff).

Employment benefits
- Job share scheme, including those at supervisory level and above.
- Flexible contract for working parents and career break scheme for up to five years for both men and women.
- Training session for staff at all levels, including women returners.

Future plans
- With a scheme called Opportunity 2000, the company intends to encourage women to more senior promotion.

BRITISH HOME STORES

Based: nationwide, head office London
Employees: 85% female

Employment benefits

- BHS do not insist managers and their families have to uproot and move to other areas to be eligible for promotion.
- The company offers flexible working contracts, including part-time, term-time and 'zero-hours' employment.
- Part-time workers receive the same benefits as full-time, pro rata.
- Maternity leave follows statutory recommendations, but BHS offers the right to return irrespective of length of service.
- A training programme, Focus on Development, is offered to all employees, including part-time and Saturday staff.

Other female-friendly employers who offer good deals to returners and working mothers include:

BBC: Offers subsidised nurseries, job sharing, flexi-working, career breaks of up to five years, working parents' advisors and holiday play-schemes. Maternity leave of 40 weeks (18 at full pay).

THE BODY SHOP: Anita Roddick comments: 'The Body Shop's commitment to the working mother is most obvious in the creche we opened at our Littlehampton headquarters. I'm amazed and embarrassed that there has been so little preparation for the future by businesses or the Government.' Offers job sharing, full-time jobs into part time, two weeks paternity leave.

BP: Offers career breaks of up to two years for both sexes, job sharing, full-time rights for part-timers, workplace creches and parental leave.

BRITISH AIRWAYS: Offers three-year career breaks, a workplace nursery at West Drayton, job sharing and flexible working at all levels.

BRITISH TELECOM: Five days paid leave to care for a sick child, 13 weeks paid maternity leave, paternity/adoption leave at managerial discretion. Plus flexible hours, job sharing, part-time and teleworking.

DENTON HALL BURGIN AND WARRENS (City law firm): Partner Gill Briant: 'Organisation and planning are essential skills that a working mother will certainly have to develop, and may make her more efficient than her male counterpart.' Negotiable career breaks, part-time working and job sharing throughout the company.

ICI: Offers 52 weeks maternity leave (full salary for 18), career breaks of up to five years for both sexes, workplace nurseries plus guaranteed places in local nurseries, flexible and part-time working and job sharing.

KINGFISHER PLC (includes Woolworth, Superdrug, B & Q, Comet): Almost half the female employees work on a part-time basis with the same holiday leave, sick pay, pension provision and bonuses as full-time workers. Offers flexi-time, term-time work and job sharing.

KMPG PEAT MARWICK (City Accountants): Head of personnel Tony Smith encourages women returners: 'They know our systems and get up to speed more effectively than a new recruit.' Offers career breaks, flexi-hours and part-time working. Creches, improved maternity conditions, childcare vouchers, returners bonus and support network are all under review.

NATWEST BANK: Head of Equal Opportunities Ann Rennie: 'The bank has a positive attitude to returners. They are a worthwhile investment.' Offers flexible and part-time work, job sharing, career breaks of up to five years.

NHS: Minister for Health, Virginia Bottomley: 'Positive action for returners is essential in the NHS where 75% of our workforce is female.' Career breaks, workplace creches, childcare allowances; job sharing, part-time and parental leave negotiable at all levels.

SAINSBURY: Offers special leave for domestic crises, workplace nurseries, career breaks of up to five years for managers, term-time and part-time work.

SECURICOR: Chief executive Henry W McKay: 'We do not wish to lose skilled staff at any level and actively encourage women to return to work.' Offers a bonus on return from maternity leave, part-time and flexible working, leave for sick children and health screenings.

TESCO: Offers up to six weeks full-pay maternity leave, job sharing, part-time jobs from full time with the same rights, career breaks of up to five years and flexible working.

W H SMITH: General manager staff and training, John Ainley: 'We will continue to develop further support.' Offers flexible working, part-time job sharing and a workplace nursery at the Swindon head office.

Fact Section

The rights and benefits explained here are the legal minimum; your employer, the personnel department or union representative will be able to tell you about any better deals your company may offer. Bear in mind that there are likely to be some changes to maternity benefits and rights in about two years' time as a result of a European directive.

Your Rights at Work

Time off: however long you have been employed in your present job, you are entitled to paid time off for antenatal care—and that includes relaxation classes. You should give advance warning of your absences, and you may be required to show your appointment card and your maternity certificate (Form MAT B1) signed by your GP or midwife confirming your pregnancy.

Qualifying period: many of the other employment rights depend on whether you've worked for the same employer for:

TWO YEARS FULL TIME (over 16 hours a week) or

FIVE YEARS PART TIME (8–16 hours a week)

by the end of the 12th week before your baby is due.

Protecting your health: working with certain chemicals or X-rays is dangerous in pregnancy, as is heavy lifting. Providing you have been with your employer for the qualifying period above, you have the right to be moved to another job.

● Your employers must offer you an alternative on similar terms and conditions to your original work. They can only fairly dismiss you if none exists. However, you will still be entitled to maternity leave and higher rate maternity pay if you would have qualified for them.

● If you have not worked for the qualifying period and are dismissed for the reasons above, you will not be entitled to maternity leave, but you will still get basic rate maternity pay if you would have qualified for it.

Maternity Pay

Statutory Maternity Pay (SMP)

This is a weekly payment for women who work during pregnancy, and is payable regardless of whether you intend to return to work.
Qualifying period
• To receive the basic minimum, you must have worked for the same employer for six months by the 15th week before your baby is due (weeks are calculated Sunday to Sunday—count backwards from the Sunday before your baby is due, or from the day if it is a Sunday). You must have worked for at least 26 weeks by the end of that week to qualify.
• You must still be employed in this 15th week (you can be on holiday or off sick).
• You must earn an average of £54 or more a week.
Basic rate: currently £46.30 a week, payable for any 18-week period after week 11 before the birth and week 11 after the birth.
Higher rate: if you have been with your employer for two years full time, or five part time by the 15th week before your baby is due, you are entitled to a higher rate of SMP, equal to $^9/_{10}$ths of your average pay for the first six weeks. After that you get the basic rate.
• Week 11 is the earliest you can receive SMP at either rate. You can work later in your pregnancy if you wish, but for every week you work later than week seven before the birth you will lose a week's SMP. If you qualify for the higher rate, your first six weeks will always be paid at this rate.
How to get it: write to your employers at least three weeks before you intend to stop work, asking for your SMP. You must also send a copy of your maternity certificate, form MAT B1; you may lose your right to SMP if you don't give three weeks' notice.

Maternity Allowance

If you don't qualify for SMP because you changed jobs during your pregnancy or are self-employed, you may be able to claim this weekly allowance, provided you have paid full rate National Insurance contributions for at least 26 weeks before the 15th week before your baby is due. Also, if you failed to give your long-time employer three weeks' notice and can't get SMP, you may be able to get Maternity Allowance for some weeks instead.

Basic rate: currently £42.25 per week, payable for up to 18 weeks as SMP (above). You won't get Maternity Allowance for any week you work.

How to claim it
• Get form MA1 from your antenatal clinic or social security office and send it off as soon as you can after you are 26 weeks pregnant. If you put it off, you may cut your entitlement. You will also need to send your maternity certificate MAT B1, and a form SMP1 from your employer if you have been turned down for SMP, but don't delay if you haven't yet received these—you can forward them later.

Sickness Benefit

If you are not eligible for either SMP or Maternity Allowance, you may be able to claim sickness benefit of £41.20 for eight weeks around the birth. If you worked and paid National Insurance contributions at some time in the last three years you may qualify. Ask at your Social Security office how to apply, and be prepared to insist—the right of pregnant women to sickness benefit is often overlooked.

Step-By-Step Guide to Protecting Your Job

You have a right to return to your own or a similar job, up to 29 weeks after your baby is born, providing:
• You have worked for your employers for two years full time or five years part time without a break by the end of the 12th week before the baby is due. (A previous maternity leave does not count as a break in service.)
• Your company employs at least six other people.
• You work until at least the end of the 12th week before the week your baby is due, unless you are sick or on holiday. To find this vital week, work back from the Sunday before your baby is

due (or the day it is due if that is a Sunday) and count back 11 Sundays.

However, you must follow all the necessary steps to protect your right to return:

• You must write to your employers at least 21 days before you leave, saying that you are going on maternity leave and that you intend to return after the birth. If you cannot give 21 days' notice, for example if you have to go into hospital unexpectedly, you must write as soon as you reasonably can.

• After your baby is born, your employer may write at any time from seven weeks after the birth asking you to confirm you are returning to work. *You must reply in writing within 14 days or you will lose your right to return.*

• Write to your employer again at least 21 days before you intend to return *giving the exact date.*

If you fulfil all these conditions you have the right to up to 40 weeks maternity leave, beginning 11 weeks before the birth and continuing for 29 weeks from the week of the birth. The 29 weeks starts on the Sunday at the beginning of the week the baby is actually born. If you give birth prematurely, you may have to bring forward the date you plan to return.

Delaying your return

• You cannot extend your leave beyond 29 weeks after the birth, unless you are ill, then you can delay going back for four weeks. You must keep your employer informed, and provide a medical certificate.

• Your employer can also delay your return for up to four weeks. You must be given the reason, and a new date for your return.

• If an interruption of work, such as a strike, stops you returning on your intended date, you can delay your return until work starts again. If the interruption prevents you giving 21 days' notice, you can delay your return for up to 28 days after the end of the interruption.

If you have problems getting any of the employment rights listed above, get advice from your trade union, Citizens Advice Bureau or your local law centre. You may be able to appeal.

Employing a Nanny: Sample Contract

This sample is based on a contract drawn up by Staff Employment
Services (SES), a campaigning organisation for the marketing and
employment industry. It is designed with nannies in mind and
although rather formal-sounding, it covers all the necessary legal
requirements and will demonstrate to your nanny that you are
prepared to be totally professional about the working relationship.
Note that points 1–8a are the legal essentials, while 9–15 provide
the basis for a good working relationship, and may well cause
problems later on if ignored! You may wish to expand point 9 into
a separate job description, which should be attached to the contract. You should always provide your nanny with a copy and keep
one yourself. If you've used an agency, it's a good idea to let them
have one too for future reference.

SPECIMEN CONTRACT

Between...And...

Employment commencement date...

This Agreement of Employment Terms starts from:...........................

Employment with a previous employer does not count as part of your
current period of employment.

---

1. Position/Job Title
2. Salary
(Details of the rate of pay per hour, day or week and how calculated.)
2a Tax and National Insurance
(Details must state if they are included in the above or not.)
2b Intervals of Pay
(Per day, week, month etc.)
3. Hours of Work
Mon........ Tues........ Wed ....Thur........ Fri ....Sat ....Sun.........
3a Total hours per week...
3b Overtime Terms
(Rates of pay or time off in lieu agreement for babysitting, cover late
arrival from work etc.)
4. Holidays and Holiday Pay (Details must include entitlement to
public holidays, any holiday pay and NI payments, and also any holiday pay on termination of employment.)
NOTE: There are no specific rules for holidays, but it is suggested
that one day's paid holiday be given per month worked up to 15 days
plus national holidays. When an employee leaves, holiday entitlement
should be taken or paid for on a pro rata basis. Tax and NI should
be deducted on all holiday pay as normal.

5. Sickness or Injury
(Details of terms and conditions of any sick pay benefits.)
6. Pension and Pension Schemes
(You are not expected to offer your nanny a pension, but the law says you must include a mention of it.)
7. Disciplinary Rules
(Areas of work ethic and attitude which might give rise to action, for example bad time keeping, failure to carry out instructions, standards of dress, incompetence, breaching employer's confidentiality.) Also state clearly reasons for *instant dismissal*, for example theft, drunkenness, negligence etc.
8. Notice
(State the days/weeks required by BOTH parties.)
8a Expiry date (if a fixed contract)
9. Duties and responsibilities (i.e. full job description)
10. Travelling expenses
(State what has been agreed, for example over petrol costs.)
11. Dress or uniform
(If optional say so.)
12. Accommodation
(Details of agreed terms, including food and arrangements for days off.)
13. Use of Services
(Include any parts of the house off limits, or machinery/equipment you don't wish your nanny/mother's help to use, when you are not there. Include her permitted use of car, telephone, TV, washing machine etc.)
14. Local Authority Taxes
(You may wish to pay part of her community charge monthly.)
15. Confidentiality
(Provide a statement along the lines of: It is a condition of employment that at all times any privileged information about my employers and their household will remain confidential and could result in instant dismissal if this trust is broken.)
You may also wish to specify in the contract any details of a trial period, also any other special arrangements such as accompanying the family on holiday, occasionally looking after other children, etc, that need spelling out clearly.

Signed
.... (Employer)
(include your address)

.... (Employee)
(include their home address)

Employing a Nanny: Tax and National Insurance

You are required by law to pay tax and National Insurance contributions if your nanny earns more than the lower earnings limits for tax and NI. These change yearly, your tax or DSS office will have the current figures. If you don't keep your side of the bargain, your nanny may lose her entitlement to various state benefits and ultimately her pension. Remember that the salary you will have discussed and agreed with your chosen nanny at interview is a net figure—you have to pay tax and both employer's and employee's NI contributions on her gross salary. You must consider this when you work out your own finances.

The paperwork

Nannies are employed under the simplified domestic PAYE scheme —when you get to grips with this you realise how difficult the real thing must be! Before your nanny starts work, contact the tax office which deals with your area and ask for the necessary paper work. You need:

P30BC(Z)—book of payslips
P12—Simplified Deduction Card
P16—the instructions, plus simplified tax tables
CF391—Non-contracted out NI contributions, with the current tax year's contributions and weekly tables
NP15—Employer's Guide to NI Contributions, available at your local DSS office if the tax office does not have it.

• It is a good idea to fill in the Simplified Deduction Card each month, at the same time giving your nanny her payslip showing her earnings and the deductions. You only have to pay quarterly, but as this can add up to quite a hefty sum it's a good idea to put aside the money each month.

• At the end of each financial year you will fill in a P37 and return it to the tax office, and you will be sent a new card and tax code for your nanny for the forthcoming year. You should also give your nanny a P60 which is a record of wages and deductions for the year. When she leaves, send the tax office her Simplified Deduction Card and start afresh with the new nanny.

• If you have problems filling in the card, particularly as a first timer, it may help to go and see your local tax officer for advice. This could save a lot of time and money later.

The DSS also run a Social Security helpline for employers (Freephone 0800 393539).

WARNING As you ask around other working mothers, you will no doubt hear of many employers who declare only part of their nanny's income to the Inland Revenue, thereby saving money on their tax bills. However, while an extremely common practice, it is an offence and a tax officer will *not* turn a blind eye, as working mum folklore would have it. If fraud is discovered, both parties can be prosecuted for the unpaid tax.

Employing a Nanny: Sick Pay

This is also rather a complex issue and is often overlooked by both employers and nannies. It should be clarified in the contract to avoid problems (see sample above). Below is a rough guide—for more help phone the Social Security office who will give you the help leaflet *Statutory Sick Pay—Rates and Notes*. Most employers will pay their nanny her full wage if she is off sick for less than a week.

• A nanny is eligible for Statutory Sick Pay (SSP) after working for you for one day, if she officially earns more than the National Insurance Contributions (NIC) lower earnings limit and is contracted to work for more than 13 weeks.

• You as employer have to pay SSP first, and then claim back 80% of the total gross SSP. You do this by deducting it from the NI contributions and tax which you send to the Inland Revenue.

• You may decide to include in your nanny's contract an undertaking to top up her sick pay to full wages, but think carefully about the implications first. If your nanny was to be incapacitated for some time (a broken leg, for example), could you afford another temporary nanny? SSP is payable for up to 23 weeks, so balance your wish to be fair with your ability to pay.

• SSP is payable after four consecutive days' illness (including the weekend) and once your nanny has been ill for three qualifying days (days on which she would normally be on duty). A doctor's note is needed after seven days' illness.

• Although you are not legally obliged to pay anything in those first four days, it makes for good working relations if you follow normal practice, which is to pay full wages.

Note on Benefits for Single Parents

• Child Benefit is £9.65 per week for your first or eldest child and £7.80 per week for each other child. Lone parents can choose to be paid weekly instead of every four weeks.
• In addition, lone parents are entitled to One-Parent Benefit for one child. This is an extra £5.83 a week.

How to claim

Get a claim form, address label CH3 and leaflet CH1 from your Social Security office, or use the form on the back of DSS leaflet FB8. For One-Parent Benefit you also need leaflet CH11. Fill in the forms and send them with the baby's birth certificate to the Child Benefit Centre, Newcastle (use the pre-paid envelope). The birth certificate will be returned.

Useful Addresses

CHAPTER 1
Maternity Alliance
15 Britannia Street, London WC1X 9JP (Tel: 071-837 1265)
Please enclose an sae for leaflets or information.
Equal Opportunities Commission (EOC)
Overseas House, Quay Street, Manchester M3 3HN (Tel: 061-833 9244)
The Return Consultancy
33 Lausanne Road, London N8 0HJ (Tel: 081-986 5105)
City Centre
32-35 Featherstone Street, EC1Y 8QX (Tel: 071-608 1338) Information and resource centre which can supply information packs on a range of employment rights and issues affecting women office workers.
For local contacts and groups:
The Working Mothers Association
77 Holloway Road, London N7 8JZ (Tel: 071-700 5771)
The National Childbirth Trust
Alexandra House, Oldham Terrace, London W3 6NH (Tel: 081-992 8637)

CHAPTER 2
Parent Network
44–46 Caversham Road, London NW5 2DS (Tel: 071-485 8535)
Operates a network of support and training groups nationally; can put you in touch with your nearest group.

CHAPTER 4
National Childminding Association/Childminding in Business! Ltd
8 Masons Hill, Bromley, Kent BR2 9EY (Tel: 081-464 6164)
Childcare Solutions
50 Vauxhall Bridge Road, London SW1V 2RS (Tel: Pat Wilkinson on 071-834 6666)

CHAPTER 5
Home Office Immigration and Nationality Department
Lunar House, 40 Wellesley Road, Croydon, Surrey CR9 2BY (Tel: 081-686 0688)

The Home Office produces a leaflet *Information About Au Pairs* and can answer individual queries, but the line is very busy.

Advisory Group for Au Pairs
c/o St Patrick's International Centre, 24 Great Chapel Street, London W1V 3AF (Tel: 071-734 2156/439 0116)
Primarily an advice and social centre for young foreigners, but may be able to put you in touch with au pairs needing a host family.

Federation of Recruitment and Employment Services (FRES)
36–38 Mortimer Street, London W1N 7RB (Tel: 071-323 4300)
Will supply a list of member agencies specialising in both nannies and au pairs. Enclose a cheque/postal order for £2.

Department of Employment
Agency Licensing Section, 2–16 Church Road, Stanmore, Middlesex HA7 4AW (Tel: 081-954 7677)
Contact if you suspect an agency of malpractice.

The Lady
39–40 Bedford Street, London WC2E 9ER (Tel: 071-379 4717)
Published Wednesdays. Classified advertisements not accepted by telephone. An advert received by first post Wednesday will normally appear in the following week's issue, but if advertising near a public holiday, it usually means an earlier press deadline.

Nursery World
The Schoolhouse Workshop, 51 Calthorpe Street, London WC1X 0HH (Tel: 071-837 7224 Fax 071-278 3896)
Published fortnightly. Will accept copy over the phone or by fax as well as by post.

National Nursery Examination Board (NNEB)
8 Chequer Street, St Albans, Herts AL1 3XZ (Tel: 0727 47636)
Can supply addresses of colleges near you running the NNEB course if you want to advertise for recent graduates. Apply in writing if you want to verify an individual nanny's qualifications.

Professional Association of Nursery Nurses (PANN)
2 St James' Court, Friar Gate, Derby DE1 1BT (Tel: 0332 43029)
Qualified nannies can join for £53 a year—a good idea since membership brings automatic insurance cover, legal advice and mediation service. Many employers pay all or part of their nanny's subscription.

Robert Barrow plc
Robert Barrow House, 24–26 Minories, London EC3N 1BY (Tel: 071-709 9611)
Specialise in nanny professional negligence insurance.

The Nannies Need Nannies Association
Co-ordinator: Lorraine Thompson, c/o 28 May Street, South Shields, Tyne & Wear NE33 3AJ (Tel: 091-454 2617)

CHAPTER 6
Daycare Trust/National Childcare Campaign
Sister organisations based at Wesley House, 4 Wild Court, London WC2B 5AU (Tel: 071-405 5617)

The NCCC is a voluntary organisation which campaigns for better daycare facilities for children. The Daycare Trust is the research side which provides free information for parents about finding childcare, improving it and advice on setting up your own community nursery, and also offers a consultancy service for employers. Its publications list includes *Daycare for Kids: a parents survival guide* (£5.50). Annual membership of the NCCC costs £10 waged, or whatever you can afford if unwaged. Members receive *Childcare Now*, a quarterly magazine about all aspects of daycare.

Working for Childcare (formerly the Workplace Nurseries Campaign)
77 Holloway Road, London N7 8JZ (Tel: 071-700 0281)

A campaigning organisation which helped bring about the abolition of tax on workplace nurseries in 1990 and now continues to lobby for better childcare facilities. It also offers practical information to individuals and organisations through a telephone advice line and various information sheets and publications on issues such as childcare and employment, workplace nurseries, campaigning for childcare. The booklet *Getting In On The Act* is an excellent guide to pressing for improvements in your local childcare provision as outlined in the Children Act. Working for Childcare also maintains a national register of workplace nurseries and employer-sponsored childcare schemes.

CHAPTER 7
Kids' Club Network
279/281 Whitechapel Road, London E1 1BY (Tel: 071-247 3009)
Working Mothers Association (see addresses for Chapter 1)
National Childbirth Trust (see addresses for Chapter 1)
Camberwell Afterschool Project (CASP)
Carmen Lindsay, 14 Badsworth Road, London SE5 0JY (Tel: 071-708 2711)
Bristol Association of Neighbourhood Daycare (BAND)
43 Ducie Road, Bartol Hill, Bristol BS5 0AX (Tel: 0272 556971)
Child Accident Prevention Trust
28 Portland Place, London W1N 4DE (Tel: 071-636 2545)
National Nursery Examination Board (NNEB) (see addresses for Chapter 5)
PGL Young Adventure Ltd
Alton Court, Penyard Lane, Ross-on-Wye, Herefordshire HR9 5NR (Tel: 0989 768768)
British Activity Holiday Association
22 Green Lane, Hersham, Surrey KT12 5HD (Tel: 0932 252994)
Consumer guide to regulated member organisations, including adventure holidays and camps for children, £3.

Independent Schools Information Service (ISIS)
56 Buckingham Gate, London SW1E 6AG (071-630 8793)
Annually updated *Summer Schools Supplement* published each spring,
price £1.

CHAPTER 8
The National Council of One Parent Families (NCOPF)
255 Kentish Town Road, London NW5 2LX (Tel: 071-267 1361)
Publishes five information packs designed for those who are either
single and pregnant, under 18, divorced or separated, bereaved, or
who have suffered a relationship breakdown. Subjects covered include
benefits, housing options, custody and guide to other more specialist
agencies. Packs are free to lone parents; either telephone or write,
specifying which pack you need. You can also consult the wide ranging
NCOPF Information Manual, with over 200 pages of essential information and practical advice. Your local library should have a copy.
The *NCOPF Return to Work* guide is also free to lone parents (please
enclose 55p in stamps). More information on NCOPF Return to Work
training courses from the training officer on the number above.
Gingerbread
35 Wellington Street, London WC2E 7BN (Tel: 071-240 0953).
Can put you in touch with your nearest self-help group, which provides a regular meeting place for parents and children. Often local
groups will be a good source of information on a down-to-earth level.
Gingerbread head office produces a range of information pamphlets
covering a variety of subjects, such as maternity benefit and lone
parent childcare.

CHAPTER 10
Time for Yourself
Courses for women, Anna Taylor (Tel: 0245 223061)
Retreats from £85.
Women's Therapy Centre
6 Manor Gardens, London N7 6LA (Tel: 071 263 6200)

CHAPTER 11
New Ways to Work
309 Upper Street, London N1 2TY (Tel: 071-226 4026)
Send an sae for membership details and literature on job sharing and
other flexible working arrangements. For Londoners, the New Ways
to Work Job Share Register might help you find a working partner.
Hackney Job Share Project
380 Old Street, London EC1V 9LT (Tel: 071-739 0741)
The project has several years' experience of devising and implementing
job shares. It can provide general information on job sharing, or help
with specific queries from individuals and employers, and can provide

training for those managing job shares or involved in recruitment. The project has also published a book, *Fair Share*, which is available from them, price £6.95.

Ownbase
Birchwood, Hill Road, South Helsby, Cheshire WA6 9PT.
A membership-based lifeline for homeworkers, with the benefits of a bi-monthly newsletter, a contact list, local groups, low-rate private health insurance and a trading directory. For an enrolment form (membership costs £17.50 a year) write to the above address.

City Centre (see addresses for Chapter 1)

For help with setting up your own business (see addresses for Chapter 12.)

CHAPTER 12
PRACTICAL HELP
For help with childcare see addresses for Chapters 1–7.

For care of the elderly:
Age Concern
Astral House, 1268 London Road, London SW16 4ER
(Tel: 081-679 8000)
Carers National Association
29 Chilworth Mews, London W2 3RG (Tel: 071-724 7776)
Counsel and Care for the Elderly
Twyman House, 16 Bonny Street, London NW1 9PG (Tel: 071-485 1550)
Crossroads Care Attendant Scheme
10 Regent Place, Rugby, Warwickshire CV21 2PN (Tel: 0788 573653)
Help the Aged (Information Section)
16–18 St James's Walk, London EC1R 0BE (Tel: 071-253 0253)

RETURNERS COURSES AND RETURN TO
LEARNING INFORMATION
City Centre
(See addresses for Chapter 1)
Dow Stoker (returners courses in the Hertfordshire area)
The Mill, Stortford Road, Hatfield Heath, Herts CM22 7DL (Tel: 0279 730056)
The North West London Regional College
Denzil Road, London NW10 2XD (Tel: 081-451 3411)
Details of all courses from central admissions.
Cambridge Regional College
Newmarket Road, Cambridge CB5 8EG
(Tel: Jackie Newton on 0223 357545)
The Pepperell Unit (run short courses for women returners and courses on Information Technology)

The Industrial Society, Robert Hyde House, 48 Bryanston Square, London WiH 7LN (Tel: 071-262 2401)
Also publish *Women Returners Guide*—a £1 information pack (from above address).
Manpower (employment services company who want to attract women returners, particularly for temping)
Head Office, International House, 66 Chiltern Street, London WiM iPR (Tel: 071-224 6688)
Women Returners Network
Ruth Michaels, Euston House, 81—103 Euston Street, London NWi 2ET (Tel: 071-388 3111)
Many **Careers Services**, run by the local Education Authority, can offer help to women returners. They are in contact with local employers, training schemes and colleges. Look in the phone book. Or you may have an Educational Guidance Service in your area, which is like the Careers Service but particularly aimed at adults returning to work or changing careers.

For more training and educational information contact your local college of Further Education or Adult Education Institute (look in phone book under 'Education'). Some Training and Enterprise Councils (TECs) run a computerised database on education and training opportunities, known as TAP. Ask at your local library to find your nearest TEC.

NEW TECHNOLOGY
'Women and Technology'
Drake House, 18 Creekside, London SE8 3DZ (Tel: 081-692 7141)
Women's Computer Centre
Wesley House, Wild Court, Kingsway, London WC2B 5AU (Tel: 071-430 0112)
Microsystems UK Ltd (National Computing Centre—run courses for women)
16th Floor, Station House, Harrow Road, Wembley, Middlesex HA9 6DE (Tel: 081-902 8881)

LEARNING LONG DISTANCE
Open University Central Enquiry Service
Walton Hall, Milton Keynes MK7 6AA (Tel: 0908 274066)
Open University Business School
(Tel: as above)
National Extension College
18 Brooklands Avenue, Cambridge CB2 2HN (Tel: 0223 316644)
Open College
St Paul's, 781 Winslow Road, Didsbury, Manchester M20 8RW (Tel: 061-434 0007)
Council for the Accreditation of Correspondence Colleges (CACC)
27 Marylebone Road, London NWi 5JS (Tel: 071-935 5391)

PRIVATE CAREERS COUNSELLING
Georgina Corscadden Associates
151 Oakhill Road, London SW15 2QL (Tel: 081-876 5502)
Return: The Women Returners Training Consultancy
33 Lausanne Road, London N8 0HJ (Tel: 081-986 5105)
Run courses for women returners and can also offer one-to-one personal careers counselling.
Careers Analysts
Career House, 90 Gloucester Place, London W1H 4BL (Tel: 071-935 5452)
Vocational Guidance Association
7 Harley House, Upper Harley Street, London NW1 4RP (Tel: 071-935 2600)
Careers Counselling Services (CV preparation and advice)
46 Ferry Road, London SW13 9PW (Tel: 081-741 0335)

SETTING UP IN BUSINESS/SELF-EMPLOYED
Women's Enterprise Development Agency
54 Bratt Street, West Bromwich, West Midlands B70 8RD (Tel: 021 525 2558)
National voluntary agency which offers help and support to women setting up or already in business, particularly low earners.
Small Firms Centre (Greater London only)
(Freefone 0800 222999)
National Federation of Self-Employed and Small Businesses
32 St Anne's Road West, Lytham St Anne's, Lancashire FY8 1NY (Tel: 0253 720911). Free 24-hour legal helpline for members.
Help and advice can also be obtained from your nearest Training and Enterprise Council (TEC). Look in your local phone book for councils in your area.

Further Reading

The Penguin Careers Guide by Ruth Miller and Anna Alston (£8.99). Examines a wide range of careers from a female perspective.

The Independent Careers Book, edited by Klaus Boehem and Jenny Lees-Spalding (Bloomsbury, £12.99). A lively, unstuffy guide, with useful addresses and a guide to independent careers in Europe.

Changing your Job after 35 by Godfrey Golzen and Philip Plumbley (Kogan Page, £7.95). Also contains an exhaustive list of careers consultants, recruitment agencies and vocational guidance centres.

How to Get Things Done by Alison Hardingham (Sheldon Press, £3.99).

Returning to Work, a directory of education and training for women by the Women's Returners Network (Kogan Page, £9.95). Lists over 1400 courses in the UK suitable for returners.

Second Chances, published annually by the Careers and Occupational Information Centre (£12.95). A comprehensive guide to education and training courses for adults. Contact COIC, Room E414, Moorfoot, Sheffield S1 4PQ (Tel: 0742 594563).

Women Working It Out by Jane Chapman, published by COIC (see address above).

Part-time Degrees, Diplomas and Certificates, published by Hobsons (£9.95) for the Careers Research and Advisory Service.

Index